The Elements
of Moral Philosophy

THE HERITAGE SERIES IN PHILOSOPHY

General Editor
Tom Regan, *North Carolina State University*

Carter: *The Elements of Metaphysics*
Rachels: *The Elements of Moral Philosophy*
Rachels: *The Right Thing To Do: Basic Readings in Moral Philosophy*

The Elements of Moral Philosophy

SECOND EDITION

JAMES RACHELS

University of Alabama at Birmingham

McGraw-Hill, Inc.

New York   St. Louis   San Francisco   Auckland   Bogotá
Caracas   Lisbon   London   Madrid   Mexico   Milan   Montreal
New Delhi   Paris   San Juan   Singapore   Sydney   Tokyo   Toronto

THE ELEMENTS OF MORAL PHILOSOPHY

2 3 4 5 6 7 8 9 0 DOH DOH 9 0 9 8 7 6 5 4 3 2

ISBN 0-07-051098-9

This book was set in Baskerville by Arcata Graphics/Kingsport.
The editors were Cynthia Ward, Judith R. Cornwell, and Tom Holton;
the production supervisor was Friederich W. Schulte.
R. R. Donnelley & Sons Company was printer and binder.

Cover art: Alexander Rodchenko.
Non-Objective Painting: Black on Black. 1918
Oil on canvas, 32 ¼ x 31 ¼".
Collection, The Museum of Modern Art, New York, Gift of the artist, through Jay Leyda. Photograph © The Museum of Modern Art, New York.

Library of Congress Cataloging-in-Publication Data

Rachels, James.
    The elements of moral philosophy/James Rachels. — 2nd ed.
        p.   cm. — (The Heritage series in philosophy)
    Includes bibliographical references and index.
    ISBN 0-07-051098-9
    1. Ethics.   I. Title.   II. Series.
    BJ1012.R29   1993   92-12498
    170—dc20

A bout the Author

JAMES RACHELS is University Professor of Philosophy at the University of Alabama at Birmingham. He is also the author of *The End of Life: Euthanasia and Morality* and *Created from Animals: The Moral Implications of Darwinism.*

Contents

Preface

Socrates, one of the first and best moral philosophers, said that the subject deals with "no small matter, but how we ought to live." This book is an introduction to moral philosophy, conceived in this broad sense.

The subject is, of course, too large to be encompassed in one short book: so there must be some way of deciding what to include and what to leave out. I have been guided by the following thought. Suppose there is someone who knows nothing at all about the subject, but who is willing to spend a modest amount of time learning about it. What are the first and most important things he or she needs to learn? This book is my answer to that question. I do not try to cover every topic in the field; I do not even try to say everything that could be said about the topics that are covered. But I do try to discuss the most important ideas that a newcomer should confront.

The chapters have been written so that they may be read independently of one another—they are, in effect, separate essays on a variety of topics. Thus someone who is interested in Ethical Egoism could go directly to the sixth chapter and find there a self-contained introduction to that theory. When read in order, however, they tell a more or less continuous story. The first chapter presents a "minimum conception" of what morality is; the middle chapters cover the most important general ethical theories (with some digressions as seem appropriate); and the final chapter sets out my own view of what a fully satisfactory moral theory would be like.

The point of the book is not to provide a neat, unified account of "the truth" about the matters under discussion. That would be a poor way to introduce the subject. Philosophy is not like physics. In physics, there is a large body of established truth, which no competent physicist would dispute and which beginners must patiently master. (Physics instructors rarely invite freshmen to make up their own minds about the laws of thermodynamics.) There are, of course, disagreements among physicists, and unresolved controversies; but these generally take place against the background of large and substantial agreements. In philosophy, by contrast, everything is controversial—or almost everything. "Competent" philosophers will disagree even about fundamental matters. A good introduction will not try to hide that somewhat embarrassing fact.

You will find, then, a survey of contending ideas, theories, and arguments. My own views inevitably color the presentation. I have not tried to conceal the fact that I find some of these ideas more convincing than others; and it is obvious that a philosopher making different assessments might present the various ideas differently. But I have tried to present the contending theories fairly, and whenever I have endorsed or rejected one of them, I have tried to give some reason why it should be endorsed or rejected. Philosophy, like morality itself, is first and last an exercise in reason—the ideas that should come out on top are the ones that have the best reasons on their sides. If this book is successful, the reader will learn enough so that he or she can begin to assess, for himself or herself, where the weight of reason rests.

*A*bout the Second Edition

Readers familiar with the first edition of this book may want to know what changes have been made. The most conspicuous change is that a chapter on the virtues has been added. There is also a new section on the Prisoner's Dilemma in the chapter on social contract theory. In addition, a few parts of the book have been rewritten, including the section on Baby Jane Doe in Chapter 1, which had to be rewritten to take account of events that occurred after the first edition was published, and the section on natural law in Chapter 4, which has been revised to provide a better account of that theory.

In other chapters, a few errors—some minor and some not so minor—have been corrected. Some of these errors were first spotted by Shelly Kagan and Edwin Curley, two philosophers who are unusually generous with their time and insight. I am grateful to them, as well as to others who have offered helpful advice: Theodore M. Benditt, who called my attention to the way virtue theory is connected with feminist thought, and Gregory E. Pence, who reviewed a draft of the chapter on virtue theory and suggested several improvements.

The Elements
of Moral Philosophy

CHAPTER 1

What Is Morality?

We are discussing no small matter, but how we ought to live.
SOCRATES, as reported by PLATO in the *REPUBLIC* (ca. 390 B.C.)

1.1. The Problem of Definition

Moral philosophy is the attempt to achieve a systematic understanding of the nature of morality and what it requires of us—in Socrates's words, of "how we ought to live," and why. It would be helpful, therefore, if we could begin with a simple, uncontroversial definition of what morality is. But that turns out to be impossible. There are many rival theories, each expounding a different conception of what it means to live morally, and any definition that goes beyond Socrates's simple formulation is bound to offend one or another of them.

   This should make us cautious, but it need not paralyze us. In this chapter I will present what I call the "minimum conception" of morality. As the name suggests, the minimum conception is a core that every moral theory should accept, at least as a starting point. We will begin by examining, in some detail, a recent moral controversy. The features of the minimum conception will emerge from our consideration of this example.

1.2. An Example of Moral Reasoning: Baby Jane Doe

In late 1983 there was a great public controversy over an infant known to the public only as Baby Jane Doe. This unfortunate baby, born in New York State, suffered from multiple defects including spina bifida (a broken and protruding spine), hydrocephaly (excess fluid on the brain), and perhaps worst of all, microcephaly (an abnormally small head, suggesting that part of the brain was missing). Surgery was needed for the spina bifida; however, the doctors who examined the baby disagreed about whether the operation should be performed. Dr. George Newman believed that surgery would be pointless because the baby could never have a meaningful human life. Another physician, Dr. Arjen Keuskamp, did not think the baby's condition was hopeless and advocated immediate surgery. (Both were pediatric neurologists.) The parents decided to accept Dr. Newman's recommendation, and refused permission for surgery. Dr. Keuskamp then withdrew from the case.

Such decisions have become relatively common in recent years, as parents and doctors have increasingly chosen not to treat hopelessly defective newborns. As medical technology has advanced, we have developed methods of "saving" babies that in earlier times would have died, and this has raised the question of whether such methods should always be used. One doctor, Anthony Shaw, writing in the *New England Journal of Medicine* in 1973, expressed his worry like this:

> Each year it becomes possible to remove yet another type of malformation from the "unsalvageable" category. All pediatric surgeons, including myself, have "triumphs"— infants who, if they had been born 25 or even five years ago, would not have been salvageable. . . . But how about the infant whose gastrointestinal tract has been removed after volvulus and infarction? Although none of us regard the insertion of a central venous catheter as a "heroic" procedure, is it right to insert a "lifeline" to feed this baby in the light of our present technology, which can support him, tethered to an infusion pump, for a maximum of one year and some months?

Dr. Shaw believed that this would be more a misuse than a use of the new technology. Similarly, the parents of Baby Jane Doe felt that aggressive treatment for their child would be pointless.

Because such cases have become common, the plight of Baby Jane Doe would not have received much attention had it not been for the intervention of third parties. Shortly after the parents made their decision, Lawrence Washburn, a lawyer associated with some conservative right-to-life groups, petitioned the courts to set aside the parents' wishes and order that the surgery be performed. The New York State Supreme Court granted that request, but a higher court quickly overturned the order, calling Washburn's suit "offensive." That court was impressed by Dr. Newman's testimony: he told the court,

> The decision made by the parents is that it would be unkind to have surgery performed on this child . . . on the basis of the combination of malformations that are present in this child, she is not likely to ever achieve any meaningful interaction with her environment, nor ever achieve any interpersonal relationships, the very qualities which we consider human.

After Mr. Washburn's suit was dismissed, the federal government got into the act. The Department of Justice filed suit demanding access to the hospital's records in order to determine whether a "handicapped person"—the infant—was being discriminated against. This suit was also dismissed, with the judge declaring that the parents' decision "was a reasonable one based on due consideration of the medical options available and on a genuine concern for the best interests of the child."

The parents did eventually agree to the use of a shunt to remove the excess fluid from the child's brain. But the major surgery, for the spina bifida, was not performed.

Was the parents' decision correct? There were impressive forces on both sides. Many people, including Dr. Keuskamp, Mr. Washburn, and the Surgeon General of the United States, did not think so. They thought that everything possible should have been done to prolong Baby Jane Doe's life. Others, including Dr. Newman and most of the judges who heard the case in court, took a different view. They thought that there was no point in prolonging the infant's life. But we are interested in more than what people happen to think. We want to know the *truth* of the matter. In fact, were the parents right or were they wrong to deny surgery to this baby?

If we want to discover the truth, we have to begin by asking what *reasons* there are for thinking that the surgery should, or should not, have been performed. What can be said to justify the parents' decision, or to justify the opposite view that what they decided was wrong? There are three main lines of reasoning to consider.

The Benefits Argument. Baby Jane Doe's parents made two assumptions, one about morality and one about the facts. Their moral assumption was that *they should do whatever is best for the baby*—they assumed that the decision should be made on that basis. Their other assumption was that, in fact, the baby's condition was so hopeless that the operation would do her no good.

For their understanding of the facts, they relied on Dr. Newman. The doctor told them that even with the best possible medical care the child would have extremely poor prospects. With surgery, she would have a 50–50 chance of surviving into her twenties, but she would be severely mentally retarded, paralyzed, epileptic, unable to leave her bed, without control of her bladder or bowels, and unusually vulnerable to such further diseases as meningitis. The mental retardation would be so severe that she would never even be able to recognize her parents. Then, perhaps sometime in her twenties, she would die. Without surgery, the baby would die sooner, probably within one or two years.

The conclusion suggested by this prognosis is that it would not serve the infant's own interests to prolong her life—sadly, it would do *her* no good. In addition, it is obvious that no one else's interests would be served by the surgery. Certainly it would not benefit the parents, who could look forward only to years of pointless labor, caring for a child who was deriving little advantage from it. And so, since no one would have benefited from the surgery, there is no reason why it should have been performed. Thus we are presented with this argument:

> **(1)** If no one would benefit from a medical treatment, then the treatment would be pointless and it need not be performed.

(2) In the case of Baby Jane Doe no one, not even the baby herself, would have benefited from surgery.

(3) Therefore, the surgery need not have been performed.

This was the principal argument in support of the parents' decision.

Was this a sound argument? That depends in part on whether the pessimistic estimate of the child's prospects was correct. Who was right about the baby's chances—Dr. Newman or Dr. Keuskamp? It is important to notice that *this kind of argument can go either way.* If Dr. Newman was right, then the argument supports the conclusion that the operation need not have been performed. But if Dr. Keuskamp was right, then the very same sort of reasoning—reasoning about what would benefit the baby—would lead to the opposite conclusion. It just depends on what the facts turn out to be.

The right-to-life activists who opposed the parents' decision believed that Dr. Newman was wrong; they trusted Dr. Keuskamp instead. But they did not oppose the parents' decision only for that reason. They also saw the struggle over Baby Jane Doe as part of a larger campaign involving more fundamental moral principles.

The Argument from the Sanctity of Human Life. One of those principles was the idea that "every human life is precious." All human life is valuable, they said, regardless of age or handicap. Thus Baby Jane Doe should have been given the surgery she needed simply for that reason.

This was the position taken by the executive branch of the federal government (although it was not shared by the judiciary). The Surgeon General, Dr. C. Everett Koop, who had been appointed to his position by Ronald Reagan because of his conservative moral views, was one of the leaders of the fight to force surgery. Speaking on television, he said: "This is a fight for a principle of this country that every life is individually and uniquely sacred." Thus we found this argument being advanced:

(1) Every human life is individually and uniquely sacred.

(2) Therefore, every individual, regardless of age or

handicap, should be given whatever medical treatment is needed to preserve his or her life.

(3) Therefore, the surgery on Baby Jane Doe should have been performed.

This argument is very different from what we called The Benefits Argument. The Benefits Argument implicitly admits the possibility that some kinds of lives may be so devoid of human qualities that preserving them is pointless—the "life" of a sick, paralyzed, bedridden person, for example, who has so little cognitive capacity as to be unable to recognize members of her own family. This argument, in contrast, invokes a principle according to which *all* human life has value, regardless of its quality.

Is the principle to which this argument appeals a good one? It certainly sounds very high-minded. But on examination it turns out to be troublesome. The trouble is that the principle seems to imply that *every human being should be kept alive as long as possible,* and that is a proposition that few thoughtful people would accept. There are many cases in which everyone (or almost everyone) would agree that keeping people alive is pointless. For example, it is widely agreed that in hopeless cases of irreversible coma, people who are being artificially maintained by the use of machines may be allowed to die by "pulling the plug." Or, to take an example closer to that of Baby Jane Doe, suppose a baby is anencephalic—born without a brain. Not even Dr. Koop believes that such a baby should be kept alive. While testifying in court, he said:

> When you talk about a baby born without a brain, I suspect you mean an anencephalic child and we would not attempt to interfere with anyone dealing with that child. We think it should be given loving attention and would expect it to expire in a short time.

Thus not even Dr. Koop would accept the principle, once its implications are made clear.

The Argument from the Wrongness of Discriminating Against the Handicapped. There is an additional argument that was used by those who disagreed with the parents' decision. From a legal point of view, the government's intrusion into the case was based on the idea that she was a "handicapped person" and that failure to provide surgery was, therefore, unacceptable discrimination against the handicapped. In seeking access to the hospital records, government lawyers cited Section 504 of the Rehabilitation Act of 1973, which states that "no otherwise qualified handicapped individual shall, solely by reason of handicap, be excluded from participation in, be denied the benefits of, or be subjected to discrimination under any program or activity receiving federal financial assistance." Since virtually every hospital in the United States receives federal financial assistance, this rule applies to them. In his public defense of the government's intervention, Dr. Koop emphasized the importance of this point: he said repeatedly that the child should not be denied medical treatment *merely because she is handicapped.* Thus he suggested this line of reasoning:

(1) It is wrong to discriminate against handicapped people.

(2) There is no doubt that Baby Jane Doe was terribly handicapped and that her parents, with the support of Dr. Newman, were denying her treatment precisely *because* of her handicaps; if she had been a "normal" child needing surgery, it would surely have been provided.

(3) Therefore, the parents' decision was wrong. The surgery should have been performed.

Is this a sound argument?

Discrimination against the handicapped is, of course, objectionable, for the very same reason that discrimination against any group is objectionable. Suppose a blind person is refused a certain job, simply because the employer doesn't like the idea of employing someone who can't see. This is no better than refusing to employ people because they are black or Jewish. To point up the offensiveness of this, we may ask *why* this person is being treated differently. Is he less able to do the job? Is he more stupid or less industrious? Does he somehow deserve the job less? Is he less able to benefit from employment? If there is no good reason for excluding him, then it is simply arbitrary to treat him in this way.

At the same time, there are *some* circumstances in which treating the handicapped differently may be justified. For example, no one would argue seriously that a blind person should be employed as an air traffic controller. Because we can easily explain why this is not desirable, the "discrimination" is not arbitrary, and it is not a violation of the handicapped person's rights.

The question to be asked about Baby Jane Doe, then, is whether a good reason can be given why, considering her "handicap," the surgery should not have been performed. And this brings us back to the matter of the infant's prospects. Dr. Newman testified that "on the basis of the combination of malformations that are present in this child, she is not likely to ever achieve any meaningful interaction with her environment, nor ever achieve any interpersonal relationships, the very qualities which we consider human." If this were so, it would not be "discriminating against her" not to perform the surgery, because there would be no good reason to do it. There is nothing arbitrary about the denial of a treatment that would do the patient no good.

Conclusion. We are now in a position to state some general conclusions about these three arguments.

The Benefits Argument, which takes the question of whether the baby would benefit to be the central issue, seems to be on the right track. The other arguments turn out on analysis to be less impressive. The principle of the sanctity of life, although it has a noble sound, looks like a red herring. When the implications of that principle are made clear, it seems unacceptable. And the argument that refusing surgery is "discriminating against the handicapped" only collapses back into the question of whether the surgery would actually be helpful. Our overall conclusion, then, is that whether the surgery should have been performed just depends on whether it really would have helped the baby. It is The Benefits Argument that identifies the relevant issue.

But if this is the relevant issue, we must return finally to

the question of who was right about the infant's prospects—
Dr. Newman or Dr. Keuskamp? The parents accepted Dr. Newman's bleak estimate of the baby's future. At the time they
had to make their decision, they could not know for certain
whether he was right. But now several years have passed and
we can, with the benefit of hindsight, answer this question
more definitively. As it turns out, Dr. Keuskamp was right. Although the surgery for spina bifida was not performed, Baby
Jane Doe did not die. She went home with her parents and
five years later she was talking, attending a school for the
handicapped (using a wheelchair), and generally doing much
better than was expected.

The parents' decision was, therefore, incorrect. Their
method of reasoning was sound, but the "facts" on which they
relied turned out to be mistaken. However, we should be careful not to infer too much from this. In the first place, this does
not mean that the parents were irresponsible or that they are
to be blamed. At the time they made their decision, they did
not have the benefit of knowing what we know now. They
were in a common predicament: often we have to make decisions when all the facts cannot be known with certainty. In
such cases we have no choice but to rely on the best information we have, and when we are not experts ourselves, this
means deciding which experts to trust. Second, this does not
mean that other parents, in other circumstances, would be
wrong to make the same decision. Other cases might have a
less happy ending. Unfortunately, pessimistic assessments are
sometimes correct.

1.3. Reason and Impartiality

What can we learn from all this about the nature of morality?
As a start, we may note two main points: first, that moral judgments must be backed by good reasons; and second, that
morality requires the impartial consideration of each individual's interests.

Morality and Reason. The case of Baby Jane Doe, like many
others to be discussed in this book, is liable to arouse strong
feelings. Such feelings are often a sign of moral seriousness

and so may be admired. But they can also be an impediment to discovering the truth: when we feel strongly about an issue, it is tempting to assume that we just *know* what the truth must be, without even having to consider the arguments on the other side. Unfortunately, however, we cannot rely on our feelings, no matter how powerful they may be. In the first place, they may be irrational: they may be nothing but the products of prejudice, selfishness, or cultural conditioning. (At one time, for example, people's "feelings" told them that members of other races were inferior and that slavery was God's own plan.) Another problem is that different people's feelings often tell them exactly opposite things: in the case of Baby Jane Doe, some people feel very strongly that the surgery should have been performed whereas others feel equally strongly that it should not have been performed. But both these feelings cannot be correct.

Thus if we want to discover the truth, we must try to let our feelings be guided as much as possible by the reasons, or arguments, that can be given for the opposing views. Morality is, first and foremost, a matter of consulting reason: the morally right thing to do, in any circumstance, is determined by what there are the best reasons for doing.

This is not a point that applies only to a narrow range of moral views; it is a general requirement of logic that must be accepted by everyone regardless of their position on any particular moral issue. The fundamental point may be stated very simply. Suppose someone says that you ought to do thus-and-so (or that doing thus-and-so would be wrong). You may legitimately ask *why* you should do it (or why it would be wrong), and if no good reason can be given, you may reject the advice as arbitrary or unfounded.

In this way, moral judgments are different from mere expressions of personal taste. If someone says "I like coffee," he does not need to have a reason—he is merely making a statement about himself, and nothing more. There is no such thing as "rationally defending" one's like or dislike of coffee, and so there is no arguing about it. So long as he is accurately reporting his tastes, what he says must be true. Moreover, there is no implication that anyone else should feel the same way; if everyone else in the world hates coffee, it doesn't matter. On the other hand, if someone says that something is *morally wrong,* he does need reasons, and if his reasons are sound, other people must acknowledge their force. But if he has no good reason for what he says, he is just making noise and we need pay him no attention.

Of course, not every reason that may be advanced is a *good* reason. There are bad arguments as well as good ones; and much of the skill of moral thinking consists in discerning the difference. But how does one tell the difference? How are we to go about assessing arguments? The example of Baby Jane Doe illustrates some of the most pertinent points.

The first thing is to get one's facts straight. Often this is not as easy as it sounds. One source of difficulty is that the "facts" are sometimes hard to ascertain—matters may be so complex and difficult that not even the experts can agree about what the facts are. As we saw, in the case of Baby Jane Doe the experts disagreed, and as a result the right thing to do was never very clear.

Another source of difficulty is human prejudice. Often we will *want* to believe some version of the facts merely because it supports our preconceptions. The case of Baby Jane Doe also illustrates this phenomenon. During the public controversy over this case, those who were predisposed to accept a "sanctity of life" ethic tended to accept Dr. Keuskamp's view of the facts, while those who took a more liberal moral position tended to believe Dr. Newman. (It is possible that even the two doctors were motivated to some extent by differing moral outlooks.) It is easy to think of other examples of the same sort: people who do not want to give money to charity often say that charitable organizations are wasteful, even when they have no very good evidence for this; and people who dislike homosexuals say that gay people include a disproportionate number of child molesters, despite evidence to the contrary. But the facts exist independently of our wishes, and responsible moral thinking begins when we try to see things as they are.

After the facts have been established, as well as they can be, moral principles are brought into play. In our discussion of Baby Jane Doe, three principles were involved: first, that we should do what will benefit the people affected by our actions;

second, that "every life is individually and uniquely sacred"; and third, that it is wrong to discriminate against the handicapped. Most moral arguments consist of principles being applied to the facts of particular cases, and so the obvious questions to be asked are whether the principles are sound and whether they are being intelligently applied. In assessing the arguments about Baby Jane Doe, we saw that there were various ways that such arguments can go wrong. Each argument was defective, but each in a different way.

It would be convenient if there were a simple recipe for constructing good arguments and avoiding bad ones. Unfortunately, however, there is no simple method available. Arguments can go wrong in an indefinite number of ways, and one must always stay alert to the possibility of new kinds of error. But that is not surprising. The rote application of routine methods is never a satisfactory substitute for critical intelligence, in any area. Moral thinking is no exception.

The Requirement of Impartiality. Almost every important theory of morality includes the idea of impartiality. The basic idea is that each individual's interests are equally important: from within the moral point of view, there are no "privileged" persons; everyone's life has the same value. Therefore, none of us can regard ourselves as having special importance. We must acknowledge that other people's welfare is just as important as our own. At the same time, the requirement of impartiality rules out any scheme that treats the members of disadvantaged *groups* as somehow morally inferior—as blacks, Jews, and others have at various times been treated.

The requirement of impartiality is closely connected with the point that moral judgments must be backed by good reasons. Consider the position of a white racist who holds, for example, that it is right for the best jobs in society to be reserved for white people. He is happy with a situation in which almost all the major corporation executives, government officials, and so on, are white, while blacks are limited mostly to menial jobs, and he supports the social arrangements by which this situation is maintained. Now we can ask for reasons; we can ask *why* this is thought to be right. Is there something about white people that makes them better fitted for the highest-paying and most prestigious positions? Are they inherently brighter or more industrious? Do they care more about themselves and their families? Are they capable of benefiting more from the availability of such positions? In each case, the answer seems to be no—and if there is no good reason for treating people differently, discrimination is unacceptably arbitrary.

Moreover, even if there were some important general difference between whites and blacks, it would still be possible that this difference did not exist in the case of many *individual* white people and black people. For instance, even if it were true (and I am not saying it is true) that whites were generally smarter than blacks, it could still be true that many individual blacks are smarter than many individual whites, and so the general difference would provide no reason for discriminating against those individuals.

The requirement of impartiality, then, is at bottom nothing more than a proscription against arbitrariness in dealing with people; it is a rule that forbids us from treating one person differently from another *when there is no good reason to do so*. But if this explains what is wrong with racism, it also explains why, in some special kinds of cases, it is *not* racist to treat people differently. Suppose a film director were making a movie about the life of Martin Luther King, Jr. He would have a perfectly good reason for ruling out Paul Newman, or any other white actor, for the starring role—obviously, such casting would make no sense. Because there would be a good reason for it, the director's "discrimination" would not be arbitrary and so would not be liable to criticism.

1.4. The Minimum Conception of Morality

The minimum conception may now be stated very briefly: morality is, at the very least, the effort to guide one's conduct by reason—that is, to do what there are the best reasons for doing—while giving equal weight to the interests of each individual who will be affected by one's conduct.

This gives us, among other things, a picture of what it means to be a conscientious moral agent. The conscientious moral agent is someone who is concerned impartially with the interests of everyone affected by what he or she does; who carefully sifts facts and examines their implications; who accepts principles of conduct only after scrutinizing them to make sure they are sound; who is willing to "listen to reason" even when it means that his or her earlier convictions may have to be revised; and who, finally, is willing to act on the results of this deliberation.

Of course, as one might expect, not *every* important theory accepts this "minimum"—as we shall see, this picture of the moral agent has been disputed in various ways. However, theories that reject the minimum conception encounter serious difficulties because they do. Most philosophers have realized this, and so most theories of morality incorporate the minimum conception, in one form or another. They disagree not about the minimum but about how it should be expanded, and perhaps modified, in order to achieve a fully satisfying account.

CHAPTER 2

The Challenge of Cultural Relativism

Morality differs in every society, and is a convenient term for socially approved habits.

RUTH BENEDICT, *PATTERNS OF CULTURE* (1934)

2.1. How Different Cultures Have Different Moral Codes

Darius, a king of ancient Persia, was intrigued by the variety of cultures he encountered in his travels. He had found, for example, that the Callatians (a tribe of Indians) customarily ate the bodies of their dead fathers. The Greeks, of course, did not do that—the Greeks practiced cremation and regarded the funeral pyre as the natural and fitting way to dispose of the dead. Darius thought that a sophisticated understanding of the world must include an appreciation of such differences between cultures. One day, to teach this lesson, he summoned some Greeks who happened to be present at his court and asked them what they would take to eat the bodies of their dead fathers. They were shocked, as Darius knew they would be, and replied that no amount of money could persuade them to do such a thing. Then Darius called in some Callatians, and while the Greeks listened asked them what they would take to burn their dead fathers' bodies. The Callatians were horrified and told Darius not even to mention such a dreadful thing.

This story, recounted by Herodotus in his *History*, illustrates a recurring theme in the literature of social science: different cultures have different moral codes. What is thought right within one group may be utterly abhorrent to the members of another group, and vice versa. Should we eat the bodies of the dead or burn them? If you were a Greek, one answer would seem obviously correct; but if you were a Callatian, the opposite would seem equally certain.

It is easy to give additional examples of the same kind. Consider the Eskimos. They are a remote and inaccessible people. Numbering only about 25,000, they live in small, isolated settlements scattered mostly along the northern fringes of North America and Greenland. Until the beginning of this century, the outside world knew little about them. Then explorers began to bring back strange tales.

Eskimo customs turned out to be very different from our own. The men often had more than one wife, and they would share their wives with guests, lending them for the night as a sign of hospitality. Moreover, within a community, a dominant male might demand—and get—regular sexual access to other men's wives. The women, however, were free to break these arrangements simply by leaving their husbands and taking up with new partners—free, that is, so long as their former husbands chose not to make trouble. All in all, the Eskimo practice was a volatile scheme that bore little resemblance to what we call marriage.

But it was not only their marriage and sexual practices that were different. The Eskimos also seemed to have less regard for human life. Infanticide, for example, was common. Knud Rasmussen, one of the most famous early explorers, reported that he met one woman who had borne twenty children but had killed ten of them at birth. Female babies, he found, were especially liable to be destroyed, and this was permitted simply at the parents' discretion, with no social stigma attached to it. Old people also, when they became too feeble to contribute to the family, were left out in the snow to die. So there seemed to be, in this society, remarkably little respect for life.

To the general public, these were disturbing revelations. Our own way of living seems so natural and right that for many of us it is hard to conceive of others living so differently. And when we do hear of such things, we tend immediately to categorize those other peoples as "backward" or "primitive." But to anthropologists and sociologists, there was nothing particularly surprising about the Eskimos. Since the time of Herodotus, enlightened observers have been accustomed to the idea that conceptions of right and wrong differ from culture to culture. If we assume that *our* ideas of right and wrong will be shared by all peoples at all times, we are merely naive.

2.2. Cultural Relativism

To many thinkers, this observation—"Different cultures have different moral codes"—has seemed to be the key to understanding morality. The idea of universal truth in ethics, they say, is a myth. The customs of different societies are all that exist. These customs cannot be said to be "correct" or "incorrect," for that implies we have an independent standard of right and wrong by which they may be judged. But there is no such independent standard; every standard is culture-bound. The great pioneering sociologist William Graham Sumner, writing in 1906, put the point like this:

> The "right" way is the way which the ancestors used and which has been handed down. The tradition is its own warrant. It is not held subject to verification by experience. The notion of right is in the folkways. It is not outside of them, of independent origin, and brought to test them. In the folkways, whatever is, is right. This is because they are traditional, and therefore contain in themselves the authority of the ancestral ghosts. When we come to the folkways we are at the end of our analysis.

This line of thought has probably persuaded more people to be skeptical about ethics than any other single thing. *Cultural Relativism*, as it has been called, challenges our ordinary belief in the objectivity and universality of moral truth. It says, in effect, that there is no such thing as universal truth in ethics; there are only the various cultural codes, and nothing more. Moreover, our own code has no special status; it is merely one among many.

As we shall see, this basic idea is really a compound of several different thoughts. It is important to separate the various elements of the theory because, on analysis, some parts of the theory turn out to be correct, whereas others seem to be mistaken. As a beginning, we may distinguish the following claims, all of which have been made by cultural relativists:

1. Different societies have different moral codes.
2. There is no objective standard that can be used to judge one societal code better than another.
3. The moral code of our own society has no special status; it is merely one among many.
4. There is no "universal truth" in ethics—that is, there are no moral truths that hold for all peoples at all times.
5. The moral code of a society determines what is right within that society; that is, if the moral code of a society says that a certain action is right, then that action *is* right, at least within that society.
6. It is mere arrogance for us to try to judge the conduct of other peoples. We should adopt an attitude of tolerance toward the practices of other cultures.

Although it may seem that these six propositions go naturally together, they are independent of one another, in the sense that some of them might be true even if others are false. In what follows, we will try to identify what is correct in Cultural Relativism, but we will also be concerned to expose what is mistaken about it.

2.3. The Cultural Differences Argument

Cultural Relativism is a theory about the nature of morality. At first blush it seems quite plausible. However, like all such theories, it may be evaluated by subjecting it to rational analysis; and when we analyze Cultural Relativism we find that it is not so plausible as it first appears to be.

The first thing we need to notice is that at the heart of Cultural Relativism there is a certain *form of argument*. The strategy used by cultural relativists is to argue from facts about the differences between cultural outlooks to a conclusion about the status of morality. Thus we are invited to accept this reasoning:

(1) The Greeks believed it was wrong to eat the dead, whereas the Callatians believed it was right to eat the dead.

(2) Therefore, eating the dead is neither objectively right nor objectively wrong. It is merely a matter of opinion, which varies from culture to culture.

Or, alternatively:

(1) The Eskimos see nothing wrong with infanticide, whereas Americans believe infanticide is immoral.

(2) Therefore, infanticide is neither objectively right nor objectively wrong. It is merely a matter of opinion, which varies from culture to culture.

Clearly, these arguments are variations of one fundamental idea. They are both special cases of a more general argument, which says:

(1) Different cultures have different moral codes.

(2) Therefore, there is no objective "truth" in morality. Right and wrong are only matters of opinion, and opinions vary from culture to culture.

We may call this the *Cultural Differences Argument*. To many people, it is very persuasive. But from a logical point of view, is it a *sound* argument?

It is not sound. The trouble is that the conclusion does not really follow from the premise—that is, even if the premise is true, the conclusion still might be false. The premise concerns what people *believe:* in some societies, people believe one thing; in other societies, people believe differently. The conclusion, however, concerns *what really is the case.* The trouble is that this sort of conclusion does not follow logically from this sort of premise.

Consider again the example of the Greeks and Callatians. The Greeks believed it was wrong to eat the dead; the Callatians believed it was right. Does it follow, *from the mere fact that they disagreed,* that there is no objective truth in the matter? No, it does not follow; for it *could* be that the practice was objectively right (or wrong) and that one or the other of them was simply mistaken.

To make the point clearer, consider a very different matter. In some societies, people believe the earth is flat. In other societies, such as our own, people believe the earth is (roughly) spherical. Does it follow, *from the mere fact that they disagree,* that there is no "objective truth" in geography? Of course not; we would never draw such a conclusion because we realize that, in their beliefs about the world, the members of some societies might simply be wrong. There is no reason to think that if the world is round everyone must know it. Similarly, there is no reason to think that if there is moral truth everyone must know it. The fundamental mistake in the Cultural Differences Argument is that it attempts to derive a substantive conclusion about a subject (morality) from the mere fact that people disagree about it.

It is important to understand the nature of the point that is being made here. We are *not* saying (not yet, anyway) that the conclusion of the argument is false. Insofar as anything being said here is concerned, it is still an open question whether the conclusion is true. We *are* making a purely logical point and saying that the conclusion does not *follow from* the premise. This is important, because in order to determine whether the conclusion is true, we need arguments in its support. Cultural Relativism proposes this argument, but unfortunately the argument turns out to be fallacious. So it proves nothing.

2.4. The Consequences of Taking Cultural Relativism Seriously

Even if the Cultural Differences Argument is invalid, Cultural Relativism might still be true. What would it be like if it were true?

In the passage quoted above, William Graham Sumner summarizes the essence of Cultural Relativism. He says that there is no measure of right and wrong other than the standards of one's society: "The notion of right is in the folkways.

It is not outside of them, of independent origin, and brought to test them. In the folkways, whatever is, is right."

Suppose we took this seriously. What would be some of the consequences?

1. *We could no longer say that the customs of other societies are morally inferior to our own.* This, of course, is one of the main points stressed by Cultural Relativism. We would have to stop condemning other societies merely because they are "different." So long as we concentrate on certain examples, such as the funerary practices of the Greeks and Callatians, this may seem to be a sophisticated, enlightened attitude.

However, we would also be stopped from criticizing other, less benign practices. Suppose a society waged war on its neighbors for the purpose of taking slaves. Or suppose a society was violently anti-Semitic and its leaders set out to destroy the Jews. Cultural Relativism would preclude us from saying that either of these practices was wrong. We would not even be able to say that a society tolerant of Jews is *better* than the anti-Semitic society, for that would imply some sort of transcultural standard of comparison. The failure to condemn *these* practices does not seem "enlightened"; on the contrary, slavery and anti-Semitism seem wrong *wherever* they occur. Nevertheless, if we took Cultural Relativism seriously, we would have to admit that these social practices also are immune from criticism.

2. *We could decide whether actions are right or wrong just by consulting the standards of our society.* Cultural Relativism suggests a simple test for determining what is right and what is wrong: all one has to do is ask whether the action is in accordance with the code of one's society. Suppose a resident of South Africa is wondering whether his country's policy of *apartheid*—rigid racial segregation—is morally correct. All he has to do is ask whether this policy conforms to his society's moral code. If it does, there is nothing to worry about, at least from a moral point of view.

This implication of Cultural Relativism is disturbing because few of us think that our society's code is perfect—we can think of ways it might be improved. Yet Cultural Relativism would not only forbid us from criticizing the codes of *other* societies; it would stop us from criticizing our *own*. After all, if right and wrong are relative to culture, this must be true for our own culture just as much as for others.

3. *The idea of moral progress is called into doubt.* Usually, we think that at least some changes in our society have been for the better. (Some, of course, may have been changes for the worse.) Consider this example: Throughout most of Western history the place of women in society was very narrowly circumscribed. They could not own property; they could not vote or hold political office; with a few exceptions, they were not permitted to have paying jobs; and generally they were under the almost absolute control of their husbands. Recently much of this has changed, and most people think of it as progress.

If Cultural Relativism is correct, can we legitimately think of this as progress? Progress means replacing a way of doing things with a *better* way. But by what standard do we judge the new ways as better? If the old ways were in accordance with the social standards of their time, then Cultural Relativism would say it is a mistake to judge them by the standards of a different time. Eighteenth-century society was, in effect, a different society from the one we have now. To say that we have made progress implies a judgment that present-day society is better, and that is just the sort of transcultural judgment that, according to Cultural Relativism, is impermissible.

Our idea of social *reform* will also have to be reconsidered. A reformer such as Martin Luther King, Jr., seeks to change his society for the better. Within the constraints imposed by Cultural Relativism, there is one way this might be done. If a society is not living up to its own ideals, the reformer may be regarded as acting for the best: the ideals of the society are the standard by which we judge his or her proposals as worthwhile. But the "reformer" may not challenge the ideals themselves, for those ideals are by definition correct. According to Cultural Relativism, then, the idea of social reform makes sense only in this very limited way.

These three consequences of Cultural Relativism have led many thinkers to reject it as implausible on its face. It does make sense, they say, to condemn some practices, such as slavery and anti-Semitism, wherever they occur. It makes sense to think that our own society has made some moral progress, while admitting that it is still imperfect and in need of reform. Because Cultural Relativism says that these judgments make no sense, the argument goes, it cannot be right.

2.5. Why There Is Less Disagreement Than It Seems

The original impetus for Cultural Relativism comes from the observation that cultures differ dramatically in their views of right and wrong. But just how much do they differ? It is true that there are differences. However, it is easy to overestimate the extent of those differences. Often, when we examine what *seems* to be a dramatic difference, we find that the cultures do not differ nearly as much as it appears.

Consider a culture in which people believe it is wrong to eat cows. This may even be a poor culture, in which there is not enough food; still, the cows are not to be touched. Such a society would *appear* to have values very different from our own. But does it? We have not yet asked why these people will not eat cows. Suppose it is because they believe that after death the souls of humans inhabit the bodies of animals, especially cows, so that a cow may be someone's grandmother. Now do we want to say that their values are different from ours? No; the difference lies elsewhere. The difference is in our belief systems, not in our values. We agree that we shouldn't eat Grandma; we simply disagree about whether the cow *is* (or could be) Grandma.

The general point is this. Many factors work together to produce the customs of a society. The society's values are only one of them. Other matters, such as the religious and factual beliefs held by its members and the physical circumstances in which they must live, are also important. We cannot conclude, then, merely because customs differ, that there is a disagreement about *values*. The difference in customs may be attributable to some other aspect of social life. Thus there may be less disagreement about values than there appears to be.

Consider the Eskimos again. They often kill perfectly normal infants, especially girls. We do not approve of this at all; a parent who did this in our society would be locked up.

Thus there appears to be a great difference in the values of our two cultures. But suppose we ask *why* the Eskimos do this. The explanation is not that they have less affection for their children or less respect for human life. An Eskimo family will always protect its babies if conditions permit. But they live in a harsh environment, where food is often in short supply. A fundamental postulate of Eskimo thought is: "Life is hard, and the margin of safety small." A family may want to nourish its babies but be unable to do so.

As in many "primitive" societies, Eskimo mothers will nurse their infants over a much longer period of time than mothers in our culture. The child will take nourishment from its mother's breast for four years, perhaps even longer. So even in the best of times there are limits to the number of infants that one mother can sustain. Moreover, the Eskimos are a nomadic people—unable to farm, they must move about in search of food. Infants must be carried, and a mother can carry only one baby in her parka as she travels and goes about her outdoor work. Other family members can help, but this is not always possible.

Infant girls are more readily disposed of because, first, in this society the males are the primary food providers—they are the hunters, according to the traditional division of labor—and it is obviously important to maintain a sufficient number of food gatherers. But there is an important second reason as well. Because the hunters suffer a high casualty rate, the adult men who die prematurely far outnumber the women who die early. Thus if male and female infants survived in equal numbers, the female adult population would greatly outnumber the male adult population. Examining the available statistics, one writer concluded that "were it not for female infanticide . . . there would be approximately one-and-a-half times as many females in the average Eskimo local group as there are food-producing males."

So among the Eskimos, infanticide does not signal a fundamentally different attitude toward children. Instead, it is a recognition that drastic measures are sometimes needed to ensure the family's survival. Even then, however, killing the baby is not the first option considered. Adoption is common; childless couples are especially happy to take a more fertile couple's "surplus." Killing is only the last resort. I emphasize this in order to show that the raw data of the anthropologists can be misleading; it can make the differences in values between cultures appear greater than they are. The Eskimos' values are not all that different from our values. It is only that life forces upon them choices that we do not have to make.

2.6. How All Cultures Have Some Values in Common

It should not be surprising that, despite appearances, the Eskimos are protective of their children. How could it be otherwise? How could a group survive that did *not* value its young? This suggests a certain argument, one which shows that all cultural groups must be protective of their infants:

(1) Human infants are helpless and cannot survive if they are not given extensive care for a period of years.

(2) Therefore, if a group did not care for its young, the young would not survive, and the older members of the group would not be replaced. After a while the group would die out.

(3) Therefore, any cultural group that continues to exist must care for its young. Infants that are *not* cared for must be the exception rather than the rule.

Similar reasoning shows that other values must be more or less universal. Imagine what it would be like for a society to place no value at all on truth telling. When one person spoke to another, there would be no presumption at all that he was telling the truth—for he could just as easily be speaking falsely. Within that society, there would be no reason to pay attention to what anyone says. (I ask you what time it is, and you say "Four o'clock." But there is no presumption that you are speaking truly; you could just as easily have said the first thing that came into your head. So I have no reason to pay attention to your answer—in fact, there was no point in my asking you in the first place!) Communication would then be extremely difficult, if not impossible. And because complex societies cannot exist without regular communication among their members, society would become impossible. It follows that in any complex society there *must* be a presumption in favor of truthfulness. There may of course be exceptions to this rule: there may be situations in which it is thought to be permissible to lie. Nevertheless, these will be exceptions to a rule that *is* in force in the society.

Let me give one further example of the same type. Could a society exist in which there was no prohibition on murder? What would this be like? Suppose people were free to kill other people at will, and no one thought there was anything wrong with it. In such a "society," no one could feel secure. Everyone would have to be constantly on guard. People who wanted to survive would have to avoid other people as much as possible. This would inevitably result in individuals trying to become as self-sufficient as possible—after all, associating with others would be dangerous. Society on any large scale would collapse. Of course, people might band together in smaller groups with others that they *could* trust not to harm them. But notice what this means: they would be forming smaller societies that *did* acknowledge a rule against murder. The prohibition of murder, then, is a necessary feature of all societies.

There is a general theoretical point here, namely, that *there are some moral rules that all societies will have in common, because those rules are necessary for society to exist.* The rules against lying and murder are two examples. And in fact, we do find these rules in force in all viable cultures. Cultures may differ in what they regard as legitimate exceptions to the rules, but this disagreement exists against a background of agreement on the larger issues. Therefore, it is a mistake to overestimate the amount of difference between cultures. Not *every* moral rule can vary from society to society.

2.7. What Can Be Learned from Cultural Relativism

At the outset, I said that we were going to identify both what is right and what is wrong in Cultural Relativism. Thus far I have mentioned only its mistakes: I have said that it rests on an invalid argument, that it has consequences that make it implausible on its face, and that the extent of cultural disagreement is far less than it implies. This all adds up to a pretty thorough repudiation of the theory. Nevertheless, it is still a very appealing idea, and the reader may have the feeling that all this is a little unfair. The theory *must* have something going for it, or else why has it been so influential? In fact, I think there *is* something right about Cultural Relativism, and now I want to say what that is. There are two lessons we should learn from the theory, even if we ultimately reject it.

1. Cultural Relativism warns us, quite rightly, about the danger of assuming that all our preferences are based on some absolute rational standard. They are not. Many (but not all) of our practices are merely peculiar to our society, and it is easy to lose sight of that fact. In reminding us of it, the theory does a service.

Funerary practices are one example. The Callatians, according to Herodotus, were "men who eat their fathers"—a shocking idea, to us at least. But eating the flesh of the dead could be understood as a sign of respect. It could be taken as a symbolic act that says: We wish this person's spirit to dwell within us. Perhaps this was the understanding of the Callatians. On such a way of thinking, burying the dead could be seen as an act of rejection, and burning the corpse as positively scornful. If this is hard to imagine, then we may need to have our imaginations stretched. Of course we may feel a visceral repugnance at the idea of eating human flesh in any circumstances. But what of it? This repugnance may be, as the relativists say, only a matter of what is customary in our particular society.

There are many other matters that we tend to think of in terms of objective right and wrong, but that are really nothing more than social conventions. Should women cover their breasts? A publicly exposed breast is scandalous in our society, whereas in other cultures it is unremarkable. Objectively speaking, it is neither right nor wrong—there is no objective reason why either custom is better. Cultural Relativism begins with the valuable insight that many of our practices are like this—they are only cultural products. Then it goes wrong by concluding that, because *some* practices are like this, *all* must be.

2. The second lesson has to do with keeping an open mind. In the course of growing up, each of us has acquired some strong feelings: we have learned to think of some types of conduct as acceptable, and others we have learned to regard as simply unacceptable. Occasionally, we may find those feelings challenged. We may encounter someone who claims that our feelings are mistaken. For example, we may have been taught that homosexuality is immoral, and we may feel quite uncomfortable around gay people and see them as alien and "different." Now someone suggests that this may be a mere prejudice; that there is nothing evil about homosexuality; that gay people are just people, like anyone else, who happen, through no choice of their own, to be attracted to others of the same sex. But because we feel so strongly about the matter, we may find it hard to take this seriously. Even after we listen to the arguments, we may still have the unshakable feeling that homosexuals *must*, somehow, be an unsavory lot.

Cultural Relativism, by stressing that our moral views can reflect the prejudices of our society, provides an antidote for this kind of dogmatism. When he tells the story of the Greeks and Callatians, Herodotus adds:

> For if anyone, no matter who, were given the opportunity of choosing from amongst all the nations of the world the set of beliefs which he thought best, he would inevitably, after careful consideration of their relative merits, choose that of his own country. Everyone without exception believes his own native customs, and the religion he was brought up in, to be the best.

Realizing this can result in our having more open minds. We can come to understand that our feelings are not necessarily perceptions of the truth—they may be nothing more than the result of cultural conditioning. Thus when we hear it suggested that some element of our social code is *not* really the best and we find ourselves instinctively resisting the suggestion, we might stop and remember this. Then we may be more open to discovering the truth, whatever that might be.

We can understand the appeal of Cultural Relativism,

then, even though the theory has serious shortcomings. It is an attractive theory because it is based on a genuine insight—that many of the practices and attitudes we think so natural are really only cultural products. Moreover, keeping this insight firmly in view is important if we want to avoid arrogance and have open minds. These are important points, not to be taken lightly. But we can accept these points without going on to accept the whole theory.

CHAPTER 3

Subjectivism in Ethics

Take any action allow'd to be vicious: Wilful murder, for instance.
Examine it in all lights, and see if you can find that matter of fact, or
real existence, which you call *vice*. . . . You can never find it, till you
turn your reflexion into your own breast, and find a sentiment of
disapprobation, which arises in you, toward this action. Here is a
matter of fact; but 'tis the object of feeling, not reason.

DAVID HUME, *A TREATISE OF HUMAN NATURE* (1740)

3.1. The Basic Idea of Ethical Subjectivism

The Reverend Jerry Falwell said in a television interview:
"Homosexuality is immoral. The so-called 'gay rights' are
not rights at all, because immorality is not right. God hates
homosexuality, and so do we. But we do not hate the homosexual; we want to help him by helping him overcome his
sin."

Falwell speaks for a large number of Americans who feel
that there is something deeply objectionable about homosexuality. In other societies, of course, people have other views.
The rulers of present-day Iran agree with Falwell and take his
view to an extreme: there, homosexuals may be castrated or
killed or both. (Falwell himself has not endorsed such an extreme view, although a leader of the Moral Majority in California did once propose capital punishment for the "crime" of
homosexuality, citing as his authority a passage in the twentieth chapter of Leviticus.) In England, on the other hand, a
more tolerant attitude is taken, and all legal penalties were re-
moved three decades ago. What attitude are we to take? One
possibility is that we might agree with Falwell and say that ho-

mosexuality is in fact immoral. Or we might disagree and say that in fact homosexuality is *not* immoral. But there is a third alternative. We might say something like this:

> *Falwell is expressing his own personal opinion, and many may agree with him. But others may have different opinions. Where morality is concerned, there are no "facts," and no one is "right." He has his opinion; others have their opinions; and that's the end of it.*

This is the basic thought behind *Ethical Subjectivism*. Ethical Subjectivism is the idea that our moral opinions are based on our feelings, and nothing more. On this view, there is no such thing as "objective" right or wrong. It is a fact that some people are homosexual and some are heterosexual; but it is not a fact that one is good and the other bad. So when someone such as Falwell says that homosexuality is wrong, he is not stating a fact about homosexuality. Instead, he is merely saying something about his feelings toward it.

Of course, Ethical Subjectivism is not simply an idea about the evaluation of homosexuality. It applies to all moral matters. To take a different example, it is a fact that Hitler and his henchmen exterminated millions of innocent people; but according to Ethical Subjectivism, it is not a fact that what they did was evil. When we say their actions were evil, we are not stating a fact about those actions; rather, we are saying that we have negative feelings toward them. Exactly the same applies to any moral judgment whatever.

We should be clear about what *kind* of theory this is. Ethical Subjectivism is not a theory about what things are good and what things are bad. It does not try to tell us how we should live or what moral opinions we should accept. It is not that sort of theory. Instead, it is a theory about *the nature of moral judgments*. It says that no matter what moral judgments we make, we are only expressing our personal feelings, and nothing more. People who accept this theory will still have moral opinions, of course—they might be in favor of gay rights or opposed to them. But whichever stance they choose, they will not believe their choice represents the "truth." They will recognize that their opinions merely represent their own personal feelings.

3.2. The Evolution of the Theory

Often the development of a philosophical idea will proceed through several stages. At first the idea will be put forward in a crude, simple form, and many people will find it attractive for one reason or another. But then the idea will be subjected to critical analysis, and it will be discovered to have serious defects. Arguments against the idea will be found. At this point some people may be so impressed with the objections that they abandon the idea altogether, concluding that it cannot be right. Others, however, may continue to have confidence in the basic idea, and so they will try to refine it—giving it a new, improved formulation—so that it will not be vulnerable to the objections. For a time it may appear that the theory has been saved. But then new arguments may be found that cast doubt on the new version of the theory. Once again the new objections may cause some to abandon the idea, while others may keep the faith and try to salvage the theory by formulating still another "improved" version. The whole process of revision and criticism will then start over again.

The theory of Ethical Subjectivism has developed in just this way. It began as a simple idea—in the words of David Hume, that morality is a matter of sentiment rather than fact. But as objections were raised to the theory, and as its defenders tried to answer the objections, the theory evolved into something much more sophisticated.

3.3. The First Stage: Simple Subjectivism

As we have already observed, Ethical Subjectivism is a theory about the nature of moral judgments. The simplest version of the theory, which states the main idea but does not attempt to refine it very much, is this: when a person says that something is morally good or bad, this means that he or she approves of that thing, or disapproves of it, and nothing more. In other words:

> "X is morally acceptable"
> "X is right"
> "X is good"
> "X ought to be done"
> } all mean: "I (the speaker) approve of X"

And similarly:

"X is morally unacceptable"
　　　　　"X is wrong"　} all mean: "I (the speaker)
　　　　　"X is bad"　　　　　　　　disapprove of X"
"X ought not to be done"

We might call this version of the theory *Simple Subjectivism*. It expresses the basic idea of Ethical Subjectivism in a plain, uncomplicated form, and many people have found it attractive. However, Simple Subjectivism is open to several rather obvious objections, because it has implications that are contrary to what we know to be the case (or at least, contrary to what we *think* we know to be the case) about the nature of moral evaluation. Let me mention two of the most prominent objections.

1. We are sometimes wrong in our evaluations. None of us is infallible, we can make mistakes; and when we discover that we are mistaken, we may want to change our judgments. But if Simple Subjectivism were correct, this would be impossible—because Simple Subjectivism implies that each of us is infallible.

Consider Falwell again, who says homosexuality is immoral. According to Simple Subjectivism, what he is saying is that he, Falwell, disapproves of homosexuality. Now of course it is possible that he is not speaking sincerely—it is possible that he really does not disapprove of homosexuality, that he is merely playing to his conservative audience. But *if we assume he is speaking sincerely*—if we assume he really does disapprove of it—then it follows that what he says is true. So long as he is honestly representing his own feelings, he cannot be mistaken.

Thus the following argument may be offered against Simple Subjectivism:

(1) If Simple Subjectivism is correct, then each of us is infallible in our moral judgments, at least so long as we are speaking sincerely.

(2) However, we are not infallible. We may be mistaken, even when we are speaking sincerely.

(3) Therefore, Simple Subjectivism cannot be correct.

2. The second argument against Simple Subjectivism is based on the idea that this theory cannot account for the fact of *disagreement* in ethics. Dan Bradley was formerly the director of the United States Legal Services Administration; he resigned in 1982 in order to "come out of the closet" and publicly acknowledge his homosexuality. (He was the highest government official to have done this, and so his declaration was widely publicized.) Bradley insists that homosexuality is not immoral. On the face of it, it appears that Bradley and Falwell disagree. But consider what Simple Subjectivism implies about this situation.

According to Simple Subjectivism, when Bradley says that homosexuality is not immoral, he is merely making a statement about his attitude—he is saying that he, Bradley, does not disapprove of homosexuality. Would Falwell disagree with that? No, Falwell would *agree* that Bradley does not disapprove of homosexuality. At the same time, when Falwell says that homosexuality is immoral, he is only saying that he, Falwell, disapproves of it. And why should Bradley disagree with *that?* In fact, Bradley would certainly acknowledge that Falwell disapproves of homosexuality. Thus according to Simple Subjectivism, there is no disagreement between them—each would acknowledge the truth of what the other is saying! Surely, the argument goes, there is something wrong here, for surely Falwell and Bradley *do* disagree about whether homosexuality is immoral.

There is a kind of eternal frustration implied by Simple Subjectivism: Falwell and Bradley are deeply opposed to one another; yet they cannot even state their positions in a way that joins the issue. Bradley may *try* to deny what Falwell says, by denying that homosexuality is immoral, but according to Simple Subjectivism he succeeds only in changing the subject.

The argument may be summarized like this:

(1) When one person says "X is morally acceptable" and someone else says "X is morally unacceptable," they are disagreeing.

(2) However, if Simple Subjectivism were correct, there would be no disagreement between them.

(3) Therefore, Simple Subjectivism cannot be correct.

These arguments, and others like them, show that Simple Subjectivism is a flawed theory: it cannot be maintained, at least not in such a crude form. In the face of such arguments, some thinkers have chosen to reject the whole idea of Ethical Subjectivism. Others, however, have worked to produce a better version of the theory, one that would not be vulnerable to these objections.

3.4. The Second Stage: Emotivism

The improved version was a theory that came to be known as *Emotivism*. Developed chiefly by the American philosopher Charles L. Stevenson (1908–1979), Emotivism has been one of the most influential theories of ethics in the twentieth century. It is a far more subtle and sophisticated theory than Simple Subjectivism.

Emotivism begins with the observation that language is used in a variety of ways. One of its principal uses is in stating facts, or at least in stating what we believe to be facts. Thus we may say:

> "Abraham Lincoln was President of the United States."
>
> "I have an appointment at four o'clock."
>
> "Gasoline costs $1.19 per gallon."
>
> "Shakespeare is the author of *Hamlet*."

And so on. In each case, we are saying something that is either true or false, and the purpose of our utterance is, typically, to convey information to the listener.

However, there are other purposes for which language may be used. For example, suppose I say to you "Close the door!" This utterance is neither true nor false. It is not a *statement* of any kind; it is a *command*, which is something altogether different. Its purpose is not to convey information; rather, its purpose is *to get you to do something*. In giving you a command, I am not trying to alter your beliefs; instead I am trying to influence your conduct.

Or consider utterances such as these, which are neither statements of fact nor commands:

"Hurrah for Abraham Lincoln!"
"Would that gasoline did not cost so much!"
"Alas!"
"Damn Hamlet!"

These are perfectly familiar, common types of sentences that we understand easily enough. But none of them is "true" or "false." (It would make no sense to say "It is true that hurrah for Abraham Lincoln" or "It is false that alas.") Again, these sentences are not used to state facts; instead, they are used to express the speaker's attitudes.

We need to note clearly the difference between *reporting* an attitude and *expressing* the same attitude. If I say "I like Abraham Lincoln," I am reporting the fact that I have a positive attitude toward him. The statement is a statement of fact, which is either true or false. On the other hand, if I shout "Hurrah for Lincoln!" I am not stating any sort of fact. I am expressing an attitude, but I am not reporting that I have it.

Now, with these points in mind, let us turn our attention to moral language. According to Emotivism, moral language is not fact-stating language; it is not typically used to convey information. Its purpose is entirely different. It is used, first, as a means of influencing people's behavior: if someone says "You ought not to do that," he is *trying to stop you from doing it.* Thus the utterance is more like a command than a statement of fact; it is as though he had said "Don't do that!" Second, moral language is used to express (*not* report) one's attitude. Saying "Lincoln was a good man" is not like saying "I approve of Lincoln," but it *is* like saying "Hurrah for Lincoln!"

The difference between Emotivism and Simple Subjectivism should now be obvious. Simple Subjectivism interpreted ethical sentences as statements of fact, of a special kind—namely, as reports of the speaker's attitude. According to Simple Subjectivism, when Falwell says "Homosexuality is immoral," this means the same as "I (Falwell) disapprove of homosexuality"—a statement of fact about his attitude. Emotivism, on the other hand, would deny that his utterance states any fact at all, even a fact about himself. Instead, Emotivism interprets his utterance as equivalent to something such as

"Homosexuality—yecch!" or "Do not engage in homosexual acts!" or "Would that there were no homosexuals."

Now this may seem to be a trivial, nitpicking difference that isn't worth bothering with. But from a theoretical point of view, it is actually a very big and important difference. One way to see this is to consider again the arguments against Simple Subjectivism. While those arguments were severely embarrassing to Simple Subjectivism, they do not affect Emotivism at all.

1. The first argument was that if Simple Subjectivism is correct, then we are all infallible in our moral judgments; but we certainly are not infallible; therefore, Simple Subjectivism cannot be correct.

This argument is effective only because Simple Subjectivism interprets moral judgments as statements that can be true or false. "Infallible" means that one's judgments are always true; and Simple Subjectivism assigns moral judgments a meaning that *will* always be true, so long as the speaker is speaking sincerely. That is why, on that theory, people turn out to be infallible. Emotivism, on the other hand, does not interpret moral judgments as statements that are true-or-false; and so the same argument will not work against it. Because commands and expressions of attitude are not true-or-false, people cannot be "infallible" with respect to them.

2. The second argument had to do with moral disagreement. If Simple Subjectivism is correct, then when one person says "X is morally acceptable" and someone else says "X is morally unacceptable," they are not really disagreeing. They are, in fact, talking about entirely different things—each is making a statement about his or her own attitude with which the other can readily agree. But, the argument goes, people who say such things *are* disagreeing with one another, and so Simple Subjectivism cannot be correct.

Emotivism emphasizes that there is more than one way in which people may disagree. If I believe that Lee Harvey Oswald acted alone in the assassination of John Kennedy and you believe there was a conspiracy, it is a disagreement over the facts—I believe something to be true that you believe to be false. But consider a different type of disagreement. Suppose I favor strict gun-control legislation and you are opposed to it. Here we disagree, but in a different sense. It is not our beliefs that are in conflict but our desires. (You and I may agree about all the facts surrounding the gun-control controversy and still take different sides concerning what we want to see happen.) In the first kind of disagreement, we believe different things, both of which cannot be true. In the second, we want different things, both of which cannot happen. Stevenson calls this second one a *disagreement in attitude*, and he contrasts it with disagreement *about* attitudes. You and I may agree in all our judgments about our attitudes—we agree that you are opposed to gun control, and we agree that I am for it. But we still disagree *in* our attitudes. Moral disagreements, says Stevenson, are like this: they are disagreements in attitude. Simple Subjectivism could not explain moral disagreement because, once it interpreted moral judgments as statements *about* attitudes, the disagreement vanished.

Simple Subjectivism was an attempt to capture the basic idea of Ethical Subjectivism and express it in an acceptable form. It ran into trouble because it assumed that moral judgments *report* attitudes; that is why it was vulnerable to the counterarguments. Emotivism was a superior theory because it jettisoned the troublesome assumption and replaced it with a more sophisticated view of how moral language works. But as we shall see, Emotivism also had its problems. One of the main problems was that Emotivism could not account for the place of reason in ethics.

3.5. Emotivism, Reason, and "Moral Facts"

As was emphasized in Chapter 1, a moral judgment—or for that matter *any* kind of value judgment—must be supported by good reasons. If someone tells you that a certain action would be wrong, for example, you may ask *why* it would be wrong, and if there is no satisfactory answer, you may reject that advice as unfounded. In this way, moral judgments are different from mere expressions of personal preference. If someone says "I like coffee," she does not need to have a reason—she may be making a statement about her personal taste, and nothing more. But moral judgments require backing by reasons, and in the absence of such reasons, they are merely arbitrary. This is a point about the *logic* of moral judgment. It is not merely that it would be a good thing to have reasons for one's moral judgments. The point is stronger than that. One *must* have reasons, or else one is not making a moral judgment at all. This is part of what the moral concepts mean. To say "It would be morally wrong to do X, but there is no reason why it would be wrong" is a self-contradiction.

If the connection between moral judgments and reasons is a necessary and important one, then any adequate theory of the nature of moral judgment should be able to give some account of the connection. It is at just this point that Emotivism fails.

What can an emotivist say about reasons? Remember that for the emotivist, a moral judgment is like a command—it is primarily a verbal means of trying to influence people's attitudes and conduct. The view of reasons that naturally goes with this basic idea is that reasons are any considerations that will have the desired effect, that will influence attitudes and conduct in the desired way. Suppose I am trying to convince you that Goldbloom is a bad man (I am trying to influence your attitude toward him) and you are resisting the idea. Knowing you are anti-Semitic, I say: "Goldbloom is a Jew!" That does the trick; your attitude toward him changes, and you agree that he is a scoundrel. It would seem that for the emotivist, then, the fact that Goldbloom is Jewish is, at least in some contexts, a reason in support of the judgment that he is a bad man. In fact, Stevenson takes exactly this view. In his classic work *Ethics and Language* (1944), he says: "*Any* statement about *any* fact which *any* speaker considers likely to alter attitudes may be adduced as a reason for or against an ethical judgment."

Obviously, something had gone wrong. Not just any fact can count as a reason in support of just any judgment. For one thing, the fact must be relevant to the judgment, and psychological influence does not necessarily bring relevance with it. (Jewishness is irrelevant to viciousness, regardless of the psychological connections in anyone's mind.) There is a small lesson and a larger lesson to be learned from this. The small lesson is that a particular moral theory, Emotivism, seems to be deeply flawed, and with it, the whole idea of Ethical Subjectivism is brought into doubt. The larger lesson has to do with the importance of reason in ethics.

Hume emphasized that if we examine wicked actions— "wilful murder, for instance"—we will find no "matter of fact" corresponding to the wickedness. The universe, apart from our attitudes, contains no such facts. This realization has often been taken as cause for despair, because people assume this must mean that values have no "objective" status. But why should Hume's observation come as a surprise? Values are not the kinds of things that *could* exist in the way that stars and planets exist. (What would a "value," thus conceived, be like?) A fundamental mistake, which many people fall into when they think about this subject, is to assume just two possibilities:

1. There are moral facts, in the same way that there are facts about stars and planets; or
2. Our "values" are nothing more than the expression of our subjective feelings.

This is a mistake because it overlooks a crucial third possibility. People have not only feelings but reason, and that makes a big difference. It may be that:

3. Moral truths are truths of reason; that is, a moral judgment is true if it is backed by better reasons than the alternatives.

This seems to be indisputable—even the emotivists recognized the need to give *some* account of the place of reason in ethics. Thus if we want to understand the nature of ethics, it is reason that we must focus on.

A truth of ethics is a conclusion that is backed by reasons: the "correct" answer to a moral question is simply the answer that has the weight of reason on its side. Such truths are objective in the sense that they are true independently of what we might want or think. We cannot make something good or bad just by wishing it to be so, because we cannot merely will that the weight of reason be on its side or against it. And we can be wrong about what is good or bad, because we can be wrong about what reason commends. Reason says what it says, regardless of our opinions or desires.

3.6. The Example of Homosexuality

Solving moral problems, then, is largely a matter of weighing up the reasons, or arguments, that can be given for or against the various alternatives. Consider again the dispute about homosexuality. Is Falwell right? The key idea is that *we may determine whether homosexuality (or anything else, for that matter) is morally acceptable or unacceptable by formulating and assessing the arguments that can be given regarding it.* If we can produce good reasons for thinking this practice is wrong and show that the arguments in its support are unsound, then we have proven it wrong, regardless of what attitude one might have. On the other hand, if a stronger case can be made on the other side, then it is *not* wrong, regardless of what one's attitude might be.

If we consider the relevant reasons, what do we find? In opposition to Falwell, it may be said that homosexuals are pursuing the only way of life that affords them a chance of happiness. Sex is a particularly strong urge—it isn't hard to understand why—and few people are able to fashion a happy life without satisfying their sexual needs. Moreover, individuals do not choose their sexual orientations; both homosexuals and heterosexuals find themselves to be what they are without having exercised any option in the matter. Thus to say that people should not express their homosexuality is, more often than not, to condemn them to unhappy lives.

If it could be shown that in pursuing their way of life homosexuals pose some sort of threat to the rest of society, that would be a powerful argument for the other side. And in fact, people who share Falwell's view have often claimed as much. But when examined dispassionately, those claims have always turned out to have no factual basis. Apart from the nature of their sexual relationships, there is no known difference between homosexuals and heterosexuals in their moral characters or in their contributions to society. The idea that homosexuals are somehow sinister characters proves to be a myth similar to the myth that black people are lazy or that Jews are avaricious.

The case against homosexuality thus reduces to the familiar claim that it is "unnatural," or to the claim—often made by followers of Falwell—that it is a threat to "family values." As for the first argument, it is hard to know what to make of it because the notion of "unnaturalness" is so vague. What exactly does it mean? There are at least three possible meanings.

First, "unnatural" might be taken as a statistical notion. In this sense, a human quality is unnatural if it is not shared by most people. Homosexuality would be unnatural in this sense, but so would left-handedness. Clearly, this is no reason to judge it bad. On the contrary, rare qualities are often good.

Second, the meaning of "unnatural" might be connected with the idea of a thing's *purpose*. The parts of our bodies seem to serve particular purposes. The purpose of the eyes, for example, is to see, and the purpose of the heart is to pump blood. Similarly, the purpose of our genitals might be said to be procreation: sex is for making babies. It may be argued, then, that gay sex is unnatural because it is sexual activity that is divorced from its natural purpose.

This seems to express what many people have in mind when they object to homosexuality as unnatural. However, if gay sex were condemned for this reason, a host of other sexual practices would also have to be condemned: masturbation, oral sex, and even sex by women after menopause. They would be just as "unnatural" (and, presumably, just as bad) as gay sex. But there is no reason to accept these conclusions, because this whole line of reasoning is faulty. It rests on the assumption that *it is wrong to use parts of one's body for anything other than their natural purposes*, and this is surely false. The "purpose" of the eyes is to see; is it therefore wrong to use one's eyes for flirting or for giving a signal? Again, the "purpose" of the fingers may be grasping and poking; is it therefore wrong to snap one's fingers to keep time with music? Other examples come easily to mind. The idea that it is wrong to use things for any purpose other than their "natural" ones cannot reasonably be maintained, and so this version of the argument fails.

Third, because the word "unnatural" has a sinister sound, it might be understood simply as a term of evaluation. Perhaps it means something like "contrary to what a person ought to be." But if *that* is what "unnatural" means, then to say that something is wrong because it is unnatural would be utterly vacuous. It would be like saying thus-and-so is wrong because it is wrong. This sort of empty remark, of course, provides no reason at all for condemning anything.

The idea that homosexuality is "unnatural," and that there is something wrong with this, has great intuitive appeal for many people. Nevertheless, it appears that this is a defective argument. If no better understanding of "unnatural" can be found, this whole way of thinking will have to be rejected.

But what of the claim, often heard from religious fundamentalists, that homosexuality is contrary to "family values"? Falwell and others like him often say that their condemnation of homosexuality is part of their general support of "the family," as is their condemnation of divorce, abortion, pornography, adultery, and so forth. But how, exactly, is homosexuality opposed to family values? It might be said that if everyone were homosexual, there would be no families because there would be no children. (After all, children are the products of heterosexual unions.) This ignores the evident fact that many homosexuals want children and are even willing to undertake a period of heterosexual activity in order to have them. But even leaving this aside, the existence of a minority of homosexuals in society hardly poses a danger to families, because homosexuals, as a group, are no greater a threat to the lives and institutions of other people than are the members of any other group. (There have always been homosexuals; but has there ever been a society in which the institution of the family was brought down or even seriously damaged by them? No.)

Perhaps there are other arguments in support of Falwell's point of view, but I do not know what they could be. The evidence at hand, however, suggests that his view, no matter how firmly held, is not supported by reason. But my main point is not about homosexuality; that is only an example, although an important one. The main point is this: in considering a question of morality, one must ask *why* a moral judgment should, or should not, be accepted. One might have strong feelings, of course, and one might choose to ignore reason and go with those feelings. But in doing so, one would be opting out of moral thinking. Moral thinking and moral conduct are a matter of weighing reasons and being guided by them. That is why, in focusing on attitudes and feelings, Ethical Subjectivism seems to be going in the wrong direction.

CHAPTER 4

Does Morality Depend on Religion?

> There is no Good save obedient behavior, save the obedient will.
> But this obedience is rendered not to a law or a principle which can
> be known beforehand, but only to the free, sovereign will of God.
> The Good consists in always doing what God wills at any particular
> moment.
>
> EMIL BRUNNER, *THE DIVINE IMPERATIVE* (1947)

4.1. The Presumed Connection Between Morality and Religion

In 1984 Governor Mario Cuomo of New York announced that
he would appoint a special panel to advise him on ethical issues. The governor pointed out that "Like it or not, we are increasingly involved in life-and-death matters." As examples, he
mentioned abortion, the case of Baby Jane Doe, the right to
die, and artificial insemination. The purpose of the panel
would be to provide the governor with "expert assistance" in
thinking about the moral dimensions of these and other matters.

But who, exactly, would sit on such a panel? The answer
tells us a lot about who, in this country, is thought to speak for
morality. The answer is: representatives of organized religion.
According to the *New York Times*, "Mr. Cuomo, in an appear-
ance at St. Francis College in Brooklyn, said he had invited
Roman Catholic, Protestant and Jewish leaders to join the
group."

Few people, in the United States at least, would find this

remarkable. Indeed, it is not unusual in this country for priests and ministers to be treated as moral "experts." Governor Cuomo was following a well-established precedent. When the prestigious National Commission for the Protection of Human Subjects of Biomedical and Behavioral Research was organized in the mid-1970s, two seats on the commission were reserved for "ethicists"; those two seats went to a Jesuit priest and a professor at the Pacific School of Religion. The practice continues today. Most hospitals in the United States now have ethics committees, and these committees standardly include three types of members: healthcare professionals to advise about technical matters, lawyers to handle legal issues, and religious representatives to address the purely moral questions that may arise. The clergy, it is assumed, are wise counselors who can be relied upon to uphold "values" and give sound moral advice when it is needed.

Why are clergymen regarded in this way? The reason is not that they have proven to be better or wiser than other people. On the contrary, as a group, they seem to be neither better nor worse than the rest of us. There is a deeper reason why they are regarded as having special moral insight. In popular thinking, morality and religion are inseparable: people commonly believe that morality can be understood only in the context of religion. So because clergymen are the spokesmen for religion, it is assumed that they must be spokesmen for morality as well.

It is not hard to see why people think there is this connection. When viewed from a nonreligious perspective, the universe seems to be a cold, meaningless place, devoid of value and purpose. In his essay "A Free Man's Worship," written in 1902, Bertrand Russell expressed what he called the "scientific" view of the world:

> That Man is the product of causes which had no prevision of the end they were achieving; that his origin, his growth, his hopes and fears, his loves and his beliefs, are but the outcome of accidental collocations of atoms; that no fire, no heroism, no intensity of thought and feeling, can preserve an individual life beyond the grave; that all the labours of the ages, all the devotion, all the inspiration, all the noonday brightness of human genius, are

> destined to extinction in the vast death of the solar system, and that the whole temple of Man's achievement must inevitably be buried beneath the debris of a universe in ruins—all these things, if not quite beyond dispute, are yet so nearly certain, that no philosophy which rejects them can hope to stand. Only within the scaffolding of these truths, only on the firm foundation of unyielding despair, can the soul's habitation henceforth be safely built.

From a religious perspective, however, things look very different. Judaism and Christianity teach that the world was created by a loving, all-powerful God, to provide a home for us. We, in turn, were created in his image, with the intention that we would be his children. Thus the world is not devoid of meaning and purpose. It is, instead, the arena in which God's plans and purposes are realized. What could be more natural, then, than to think that "morality" is a part of the religious view of the world, whereas the atheist's view of the world—as delineated by Russell—has no place for values?

In discussing the connection (or lack of connection) between morality and religion, I will focus on one religion in particular, Christianity. There are, of course, other world religions that have been equally important. However, in our society most people embrace some form of Christianity, and when "religion and morals" are discussed, it is Christianity that people most often have in mind.

4.2. The Divine Command Theory

In both the Jewish and Christian traditions, God is presented as a lawgiver who has created us, and the world we live in, for a purpose. That purpose is not completely understood, but much has been revealed through the prophets, the Holy Scriptures, and the church. These sources teach that, to guide us in righteous living, God has promulgated rules that we are to obey. He does not compel us to obey them. We were created as free agents, so we may choose to accept or to reject his commandments. But if we are to live as we *should* live, we must follow God's laws. This, it is said, is the essence of morality.

This line of thought has been elaborated by some theologians into a theory about the nature of right and wrong, known as the *Divine Command Theory*. Essentially, this theory says that "morally right" means "commanded by God," and "morally wrong" means "forbidden by God."

From a theoretical point of view, this conception has a number of pleasing features. It immediately solves the old problem about the subjectivity/objectivity of ethics. According to this theory, ethics is not merely a matter of personal feelings or social custom. Whether something is right or wrong is a perfectly objective matter: it is right if God commands it, wrong if God forbids it. Moreover, the Divine Command Theory suggests an answer to the perennial question of why anyone should bother with morality. Why not just look out for one's own interests? If immorality is the violation of God's commandments, there is an easy answer: on the day of final reckoning, you will be held accountable.

There are, however, serious problems for the theory. Of course, atheists would not accept it, because they do not believe that God exists. But the problems that arise are not merely problems for atheists. There are difficulties even for believers. The main problem was first noted by Plato, the Greek philosopher who lived 400 years before the birth of Jesus.

Plato's writings were in the form of dialogues, usually between Socrates and one or more interlocutors. In one of these dialogues, the *Euthyphro*, there is a discussion concerning whether "right" can be defined as "that which the gods command." Socrates is skeptical and asks: *Is conduct right because the gods command it, or do the gods command it because it is right?* It is one of the most famous questions in the history of philosophy. The contemporary British philosopher Antony Flew suggests that "one good test of a person's aptitude for philosophy is to discover whether he can grasp its force and point."

The point is this. If we accept the theological conception of right and wrong, we are caught in a dilemma. Socrates's question asks us to clarify what we mean. There are two things we might mean, and both options lead to trouble.

1. First, we might mean that conduct is right *because God commands it.* For example, according to Exodus 20:16, God

commands us to be truthful. On this option, the *reason* we should be truthful is simply that God requires it. Apart from the divine command, truth telling is neither good nor bad. It is God's command that *makes* truthfulness right.

But this leads to trouble, for it represents God's commands as arbitrary. It means that God could have given *different* commands just as easily. He could have commanded us to be liars, and then lying, and not truthfulness, would be right. (You may be tempted to reply: "But God would never command us to be liars!" But why not? If he did endorse lying, God would not be commanding us to do wrong, because his command would make lying right.) Remember that on this view, honesty was not right *before* God commanded it. Therefore, he could have had no more reason to command it than its opposite; and so, from a moral point of view, his command is perfectly arbitrary.

Moreover, on this view, the doctrine of the goodness of God is reduced to nonsense. It is important to religious believers that God is not only all-powerful and all-knowing, but that he is also *good*; yet if we accept the idea that good and bad are defined by reference to God's will, this notion is deprived of any meaning. What could it mean to say that God's commands are good? If "X is good" simply means "X is commanded by God," then "God's commands are good" would mean only "God's commands are commanded by God"—an empty truism. In his *Discourse on Metaphysics* (1686) Leibniz put the point very clearly:

> So in saying that things are not good by any rule of goodness, but sheerly by the will of God, it seems to me that one destroys, without realizing it, all the love of God and all his glory. For why praise him for what he has done if he would be equally praiseworthy in doing exactly the contrary?

Thus if we choose the first of Socrates's two options, we are stuck with consequences that even the most religious people must find unacceptable.

2. There is a way to avoid these troublesome consequences. We can take the second of Socrates's options. We

need not say that right conduct is right because God commands it. Instead, we may say that God commands right conduct *because it is right*. God, who is infinitely wise, realizes that truthfulness is far better than deceitfulness, and so he commands us to be truthful; he sees that killing is wrong, and so he commands us not to kill; and so on for all the commandments.

If we take this option, we avoid the troublesome consequences that plagued the first alternative. God's commands turn out to be not at all arbitrary; they are the result of his wisdom in knowing what is best. And the doctrine of the goodness of God is preserved: to say that his commands are good means that he commands only what, in perfect wisdom, he sees to be the best. But this option leads to a different problem, which is equally troublesome for the theological conception of right and wrong: indeed, in taking this option, we have virtually *abandoned* the theological conception of right and wrong.

If we say that God commands us to be truthful *because* truthfulness is right, then we are admitting that there is some standard of right and wrong that is independent of God's will. We are saying that God *sees* or *recognizes* that truthfulness is right: this is very different from his *making* it right. The rightness exists prior to and independent of God's command, and it is the reason for the command. Thus if we want to know why we should be truthful, the reply "Because God commands it" will not take us very far. We may still ask "But why does God command it?" and the answer to *that* question will provide the underlying reasons why truthfulness is a good thing.

All this may be summarized in the following argument:

(1) Suppose God commands us to do what is right. Then *either* (a) the right actions are right because he commands them *or* (b) he commands them because they are right.

(2) If we take option (a), then God's commands are, from a moral point of view, arbitrary; moreover, the doctrine of the goodness of God is rendered meaningless.

(3) If we take option (b), then we have admitted there is a standard of right and wrong that is independent of God's will.

(4) Therefore, we must *either* regard God's commands as arbitrary, and give up the doctrine of the goodness of God, *or* admit that there is a standard of right and wrong that is independent of his will, and give up the theological definitions of right and wrong.

(5) From a religious point of view, it is undesirable to regard God's commands as arbitrary or to give up the doctrine of the goodness of God.

(6) Therefore, even from a religious point of view, a standard of right and wrong that is independent of God's will must be accepted.

Many religious people believe that they should accept a theological conception of right and wrong because it would be impious not to do so. They feel, somehow, that if they believe in God, they *should* think that right and wrong are to be defined ultimately in terms of his will. But this argument suggests otherwise: it suggests that, on the contrary, the Divine Command Theory of right and wrong itself leads to impious results, so that a pious person should *not* accept it. And in fact, some of the greatest theologians, such as St. Thomas Aquinas (ca. 1225–1274), rejected the theory for just this reason.

4.3. The Theory of Natural Law

The argument presented above suggests that right and wrong cannot be defined in terms of God's will. Although this may seem to be an antireligious conclusion, many of the great theologians of the church agree with it. In the history of Christian thought, the dominant theory of ethics is not the Divine Command Theory. The dominant theory is the *Theory of Natural Law*. This theory has three main parts.

1. The theory rests upon a certain view of what the world is like. The natural world is not regarded merely as a realm of facts, devoid of value and purpose. Instead, the world is conceived to be a rational order with values and purposes built into its very nature.

This way of thinking about the world derives from the Greeks. Aristotle, perhaps the greatest of the ancient philosophers, believed that everything that exists serves some purpose, and that we can never fully understand a thing until we understand what it is *for*. Consider the parts of biological organisms: eyes are for seeing, wings are for flying, legs are for walking, and so on. But in Aristotle's view the point applies equally well to inanimate nature. One of his favorite examples is the question of why it rains. The fact that the rain helps plants to grow is not, he says, a mere coincidence. The rain falls *in order* to provide the water that plants need. It is part of the rational plan of nature.

The Christian thinkers of the Middle Ages found Aristotle's world-view to be perfectly congenial. If nature manifests value and purpose, this could be seen easily enough as God's value and purpose. After all, God was said to have designed the world and everything in it. Therefore, the rational plan of nature was simply the order that God established when the world was created.

2. A corollary of this way of thinking is that "the laws of nature" not only describe how things *are*, they specify *how things ought to be* as well. Things are as they ought to be when they are serving their natural purposes. When they do not, or cannot, serve those purposes, things have gone wrong. Eyes that cannot see are defective, and drought is a natural evil— the badness of both is explained by reference to natural law. But there are also implications for human action. Moral rules are now viewed as deriving from the laws of nature. Some ways of behaving are said to be "natural" and some are "unnatural"; and "unnatural" acts are said to be morally wrong.

Consider, for example, the duty of beneficence. We are morally required to be concerned for our neighbor's welfare as well as for our own. Why? A natural law theorist would say that beneficence is natural for us, considering the kind of creatures we are. We are by our very nature social creatures who want and need the company of other people, and it is part of our natural makeup that we care about others. Someone who does not care at all for others—who *really* does not care, through and through—is seen as deranged, in the terms of modern psychology, as a sociopath. His personality is defective, just as eyes are defective if they cannot see. And, it might be added, this is true because we were created by God, with a specific "human" nature, as part of his overall plan for the world.

The endorsement of beneficence is relatively uncontroversial. Natural law theory has also been used, however, to support other moral conclusions that are much more contentious. Religious thinkers have traditionally opposed "deviant" sexual practices, and the theoretical justification of their opposition has come more often than not from natural law theory. If everything has a natural purpose, what is the purpose of sex? The obvious answer seems to be procreation. Sexual activity that is not connected with making babies can therefore be viewed as "unnatural," and so such practices as masturbation, oral sex, and sex while using contraceptives— not to mention gay sex—can be condemned for this reason. This way of thinking about sex dates back at least to St. Augustine in the fourth century, and it is explicit in the writings of St. Thomas Aquinas. (For a brief critical discussion of this argument about sex, see section 3.6 in this book.) The moral theology of the Catholic Church is based on natural law theory. This line of thought lies behind its whole sexual ethic.

Outside the Catholic Church, the Theory of Natural Law has few advocates today. It is generally rejected for two reasons. First, it seems to involve a confusion of "is" and "ought." In the eighteenth century David Hume pointed out that what *is* the case and what *ought to be* the case are logically different notions, and no conclusion about one follows from the other. We can say, for example, that people *are* naturally disposed to be beneficent, but it does not follow from this that they *should be* beneficent. Similarly, it may be that sex *does* produce babies, but it does not follow that sex *ought* or *ought not* to be engaged in only for that purpose. Facts are one thing; values are another. The Theory of Natural Law seems to conflate them.

Second, the Theory of Natural Law has gone out of fashion—although that does not, of course, prove it is false—because the view of the world on which it rests is out of keeping with modern science. Scientists from Galileo to Darwin have produced explanations of natural phenomena that make no reference to values or purposes. The rain falls, according to modern meteorology, only because of the impersonal operation of physical laws. If this benefits the plants, it is only because they have evolved by the laws of natural selection in a rainy climate. The rain does not fall *in order* to make anything happen; what happens just happens, fortuitously, in consequence of the laws of cause and effect. This is no less true of birds' wings and people's brains. All organisms, including people, have their particular characteristics not because it is the way they "ought" to be but because they are all products of natural selection.

Thus modern science gives us a picture of the world as a realm of facts, where the only "natural laws" are the laws of physics, chemistry, and biology, working blindly and without purpose. Whatever values may be, they are not part of the natural order. To the extent that one accepts the world-view of modern science, then, one will be skeptical of the Theory of Natural Law. It is no accident that the theory was a product, not of modern thought, but of the Middle Ages.

3. The third part of the theory may be regarded as somewhat independent of the first two. How, according to this theory, are we to go about determining what is right and what is wrong? The Divine Command Theory says that, in order to determine what is right, we must consult God's commandments. The Theory of Natural Law gives a very different answer. According to this theory, moral judgments are "dictates of reason." The "natural laws" that specify what we should do are laws of reason, which we are able to grasp because God has made us rational beings. The best thing to do in any circumstance, therefore, is whatever course of conduct has the best reasons on its side.

This means that the religious believer has no special access to moral truth. The believer and the nonbeliever are in exactly the same position. God has made all people rational, not just believers; and so for believer and nonbeliever alike, making a responsible moral judgment is a matter of listening to reason and following its directives. They function as moral agents in the same way, even though the nonbelievers' lack of faith prevents them from realizing that God is the author of the rational order in which they participate and which their moral judgments express.

The most influential of the natural-law theorists was, once again, St. Thomas Aquinas. Aquinas, whose thought is regarded as authoritative within the Catholic tradition, said that the moral life is the life lived "according to reason." In his great work the *Summa Theologica*, he wrote:

> Its moral nature is stamped on a human act by its object taken with reference to the principles of moral activity, that is according to the pattern of life as it should be lived according to the reason. If the object as such implies what is in accord with the reasonable order of conduct, then it will be a good kind of action; for instance, to assist somebody in need. If, on the other hand, it implies what is repugnant to reason, then it will be a bad kind of action; for instance, to appropriate to oneself what belongs to another. But it may happen that the object does not immediately involve the reasonable plan of life one way or the other, and then it is an action morally indifferent of its kind; for instance, to go for a walk or to pick up a straw.

Acting reasonably, he emphasizes, is not to be contrasted with acting as a Christian, for they are the same thing:

> To disparage the dictate of reason is equivalent to condemning the command of God.

This means that, where morality is concerned, the duty of a Christian is no different from the duty of anyone else: it is to think through as carefully as possible the reasons for and against various courses of conduct, and to conform one's conduct to the plan that seems most reasonable. Again, Aquinas says:

> Conscience is the dictate of reason. . . . Every judgment of conscience, be it right or wrong, be it about things evil in themselves or morally indifferent, is obligatory, in such wise that he who acts against his conscience always sins.

Thus the Theory of Natural Law—or at least, this part of the theory—leaves morality with about the same relation to religion that science has to religion. Science is autonomous. It has its own questions, its own methods of answering them, and its own standards of truth. Yet even though science is autonomous, religious people can still understand its findings in their own way. They can regard science as providing information about how God chose to arrange things: if the earth is not at the center of the universe, then God created a nongeocentric universe; if humankind is the product of a long evolutionary process, then God has created us by initiating that process. Science is independent in the sense that religious belief does not enter into the practice of science and the results of scientific investigation are religiously "neutral." The religious interpretation of those results is an after-the-fact addition—of vital interest to believers, but something that can be ignored by nonbelievers.

The Theory of Natural Law suggests that morality can be understood in the same way. Morality is autonomous. It has its own questions, its own methods of answering them, and its own standards of truth. To the moral agent intent on discovering what she should do, religious considerations are not to the point. What she wants to know is: What are the reasons for and against the various options? What do reason and conscience require of me? Believers and nonbelievers may approach these questions in the same way, and if both are conscientious and rational, they may arrive at the same answers. However, they will part company when they begin to theorize about the *nature* of what they have been doing. The believer may regard the results of this inquiry as revealing God's will—the voice of conscience, she will say, is the voice of God, and it is too bad that the nonbeliever does not realize this.

This approach leaves morality independent, in the sense that religious belief does not affect the calculation of what is best and the results of moral inquiry are religiously "neutral." The religious interpretation of conscience as the voice of God is an after-the-fact addition—of vital interest to believers, but something that can be ignored by nonbelievers. In this way, even though they disagree about religion, believers and nonbelievers nevertheless inhabit the same moral universe.

4.4. Christianity and the Problem of Abortion

Some religious people may find the preceding discussion unsatisfying. It may seem at best puzzling and at worst far too abstract to have any bearing on their actual moral lives. For them, the connection between morality and religion is an immediate, practical matter that centers on particular moral issues. Christians often say that, *as Christians*, they are committed to specific views on specific issues. It doesn't matter whether right and wrong are "defined" in terms of God's will: whatever the merits of such abstract theories, there are still the moral teachings of one's religion about particular issues. The teachings of the Scriptures and the church are regarded by believers as authoritative, determining the moral positions they must take. Thus, in the debate over abortion, for example, many believers think that they have no choice but to oppose it, because it is condemned both by the church and (they assume) by the Scriptures.

Are there, in fact, distinctively "Christian" positions on major moral issues, which believers are bound to accept? If so, are those positions different from the views that other people might reach simply by trying to reason out the best thing to do? The rhetoric of the pulpit, increasingly heard in political debate as well, suggests that the answer to both questions is yes. But there are several reasons to think that the answer, in both cases, is no.

In the first place, it is often difficult to find specific moral guidance in the Scriptures. Our problems are not the same as the problems faced by the Jews and the early Christians many centuries ago—thus it is not surprising that the Scriptures might be silent about moral issues that to us seem quite urgent. The Bible does contain a number of general precepts, such as the injunctions to love one's neighbor and to treat others as one would wish to be treated oneself, that might be thought relevant to a variety of issues. But useful as those precepts might be, they do not yield definite answers about exactly what position one should take on a host of matters such as abortion, the rights of workers, the funding of education, the extinction of species, and so forth. Moreover, in many instances the Scriptures and church tradition are ambiguous; authorities disagree, leaving the believer in the awkward position of having to choose which element of the tradition to accept and which authority to believe.

The result is that the relation between an individual's religious views and moral commitments may be a good bit more tenuous than even he or she realizes. The following is a common pattern: The Christian tradition may be ambiguous about a specific issue; within the tradition, there may be elements that support both sides. But because a particular believer feels so strongly about the issue, he or she will emphasize the elements of the tradition that support the favored moral view, while ignoring its other elements. Then, without quite realizing what has happened, he or she will conclude, quite sincerely, that Christianity *mandates* the favored moral position.

Thus when people claim that their moral views are derived from their religious commitments, they are often mistaken. In reality, something very different is going on. They are making up their minds about the moral issues first and then interpreting the Scriptures, or church tradition, in such a way as to support the moral conclusion they have already reached. Of course this does not happen in every case, but it seems fair to say that it happens often. A case in point is the issue of abortion.

In the current debate over the morality of abortion, religious issues are never far from the center of discussion. Religious conservatives hold that the fetus is a human being from the moment of conception, and so they say killing it is really a form of murder. They do not believe it should be the mother's choice whether to have an abortion, because that would be like saying she is free to commit murder.

The key premise in the conservatives' argument is that the fetus is a human being from the moment of conception. The fertilized ovum is not merely a *potential* human being but an *actual* human being with a full-blown right to life. Liberals, of course, deny this—they say that, at least during the early weeks of pregnancy, the embryo is something less than a full-fledged human being.

The debate over the status of the fetus is enormously complicated, but what concerns us here is just one small part of it. How do conservatives try to support their view that the fetus is, from the moment of conception, a human being? What evidence do they offer for this position? Often, they appeal to religious authority: they say that, regardless of how secular thought might view the fetus, the *Christian* view is that the fetus is a human being from its very beginning.

Now what makes this the "Christian" view? One might appeal (a) to the Scriptures, or (b) to church tradition.

a. It is difficult to derive a prohibition of abortion from either the Jewish or the Christian Scriptures. The Bible does not speak plainly on the matter. There are certain passages, however, that are often quoted by religious conservatives because they seem to suggest that fetuses have full human status. One of the most frequently cited passages is from the first chapter of Jeremiah, in which God is quoted as saying: "Before I formed you in the womb I knew you, and before you were born I consecrated you." These words are presented as though they were God's own endorsement of the conservative position: they are taken to mean that the unborn, as well as the born, are "consecrated" to God.

But the words are taken out of context. Suppose we read the whole passage in which they appear. Taken in context, they obviously mean something quite different:

> Now the word of the Lord came to me saying, "Before I formed you in the womb I knew you, and before you were born I consecrated you; I appointed you a prophet to the nations."
>
> Then I said, "Ah, Lord God! Behold, I do not know how to speak, for I am only a youth." But the Lord said to me,
>
> "Do not say, 'I am only a youth,' for to all to whom I send you you shall go, and whatever I command you you shall speak. Be not afraid of them, for I am with you to deliver you," says the Lord.

What is being discussed here is not abortion, the sanctity of fetal life, or anything of the kind. In this passage, Jeremiah is asserting his authority as a prophet. He is saying, "God authorized me to speak for him; even though I resisted, he commanded me to speak." But Jeremiah puts the point in a more poetic way than that; he has God saying that God had intended him to be a prophet even before Jeremiah was born.

This often happens when the Scriptures are cited in connection with controversial moral issues. A few words are lifted from a passage that is clearly concerned with something entirely different from the issue at hand, and those words are then construed in a way that supports the favored moral position. When this happens, is it accurate to say that the person is "following the moral teachings of the Bible"? Or is it more accurate to say that he or she is searching the Scriptures for support of a moral view he or she *already* happens to think is right, and reading the desired conclusion *into* the Scriptures? If the latter, it suggests an especially arrogant attitude—an attitude that assumes God himself must share one's moral opinions. In the case of the passage from Jeremiah, it is hard to see how an impartial reader could think the words have anything to do with abortion, even by implication.

The scriptural passage that comes closest to making a specific judgment about the moral status of fetuses occurs in the 21st chapter of Exodus. This chapter is part of a detailed description of the law of the ancient Israelites. Here the penalty for murder is said to be death; however, it is also said that if a pregnant woman is caused to have a miscarriage, the penalty is only a fine, to be paid to her husband. Murder was not a category that included fetuses. Clearly, the Israelites regarded fetuses as something less than full human beings.

b. Even if there is no scriptural basis for it, the contemporary church's stand is strongly antiabortion. The typical churchgoer will hear ministers, priests, and bishops denouncing abortion in the strongest terms, claiming all the while to express the "Christian" view. It is no wonder, then, that many people feel that their religious commitment binds them to oppose abortion.

But it is worth noting that the church has not always taken this view. In fact, the idea that the fetus is a human being "from the moment of conception" is a relatively new idea, even within the Christian church. St. Thomas Aquinas held that an embryo does not have a soul until several weeks into the pregnancy. Aquinas accepted Aristotle's view that the soul is the "substantial form" of man. We need not go into this somewhat technical notion, except to note that one consequence of it is that one cannot have a human soul until one's body has a recognizably human shape. Aquinas knew that a human embryo does not have a human shape "from the moment of conception," and he drew the indicated conclusion.

Aquinas's view of the matter was officially accepted by the church at the Council of Vienne in 1312, and to this day it has never been officially repudiated.

However, in the seventeenth century, a curious view of fetal development began to be accepted, and this had unexpected consequences for the Catholic view of abortion. Peering through primitive microscopes at fertilized ova, some scientists imagined that they saw tiny, perfectly formed people. They called the little person a "homunculus," and the idea took hold that from the very beginning the human embryo is a fully formed creature that needs only to get bigger and bigger until it is ready to be born.

If the embryo has a human shape from the moment of conception, then it follows, according to Aristotle's and Aquinas's philosophy, that it can have a human soul from the moment of conception. The church drew this conclusion and adopted the conservative view of abortion. The "homunculus," it said, is clearly a human being, and so it is wrong to kill it.

However, as our understanding of human biology progressed, scientists began to realize that this view of fetal development was wrong. There is no homunculus; that was only an invention of mistaken science. Today we know that Aquinas's original assumption was right—embryos start out as a cluster of cells; "human form" comes later. But when the biological error was corrected, the church's moral view did not revert to the older, more consistent position. Having adopted the theory that the fetus is a human being "from the moment of conception," the church did not let it go and held fast to the conservative view of abortion. The Council of Vienne notwithstanding, it has held that view to this day.

Because the church did not traditionally regard abortion as immoral, Western law (which developed under the church's influence) did not traditionally treat abortion as a crime. Under the English common law, abortion was tolerated even if performed late in the pregnancy. In the United States, there were no laws prohibiting it until well into the nineteenth century. Thus when the U.S. Supreme Court declared the absolute prohibition of abortion to be unconstitutional in 1973, the Court was not overturning a long tradition of moral and legal opinion. It was only restoring a legal situation that had always existed until quite recently.

The purpose of reviewing this history is not to suggest that the church's position is wrong, or even that it is irrational (although its official view of the nature of the soul, taken together with what we know of biology, does seem inconsistent with its moral position). I want to make a different point. The point is that church tradition, or the position taken by the great thinkers of the church, does *not* speak unequivocally against abortion. Of course a person might think that abortion is wrong and seek support for this view in those elements of the tradition that agree. But this is very different from concluding that abortion is wrong *because* one's religious faith mandates such a view. In this instance, as in many instances, people's moral convictions are not so much derived from their religion as superimposed on it.

The various arguments in this chapter point to a common conclusion. Right and wrong are not to be defined in terms of God's will; morality is a matter of reason and conscience, not religious faith; and in any case, religious considerations do not provide definitive solutions to the specific moral problems that confront us. Morality and religion are, in a word, different. But it should be emphasized, one last time, that this conclusion has not been reached by questioning the validity of religion. The arguments we have considered do not assume that Christianity (or any other theological system) is false; they merely show that even if such a system is true, morality remains an independent matter.

CHAPTER 5

Psychological Egoism

But the age of chivalry is gone. That of sophisters, economists, and calculators, has succeeded.
EDMUND BURKE, *REFLECTIONS ON THE REVOLUTION IN FRANCE* (1790)

5.1. Is Unselfishness Possible?

Morality and psychology go together. Morality tells us what we *ought* to do; but there is little point to it if we are not *able* to do as we ought. It may be said that we should love our enemies; but that is empty talk unless we are capable of loving them. A sound morality must be based on a realistic conception of what is possible for human beings.

Almost every system of morality recommends that we behave unselfishly. It is said that we should take the interests of other people into account when we are deciding what to do: we should not harm other people; in fact, we should try to be helpful to them whenever possible—even if it means forgoing some advantage for ourselves.

But are we capable of being unselfish? There is a theory of human nature, once widely held among philosophers, psychologists, and economists, and still held by many ordinary people, that says we are not capable of unselfishness. According to this theory, known as *Psychological Egoism,* each person is so constituted that he will look out only for his *own* interests. Therefore, it is unreasonable to expect people to behave "altruistically." Human nature being what it is, people will respond to the needs of others only when there is something in it for themselves. Pure altruism is a myth—it simply does not exist.

If this view is correct, people are very different from what we usually suppose. Of course, no one doubts that each of us cares very much about his own welfare. But we also believe that we care about others as well, at least to some extent. If Psychological Egoism is correct, this is only an illusion—in the final analysis, we care nothing for other people. Because it so contradicts our usual conception of ourselves, this is a shocking doctrine. Why have so many believed it to be true?

5.2. The Strategy of Reinterpreting Motives

Psychological Egoism seems to fly in the face of the facts. It is tempting to respond to it by saying something like this: "*Of course* people sometimes act unselfishly. Jones gave up a trip to the movies, which he would have enjoyed very much, so that he could contribute the money for famine relief. Brown spends his free time doing volunteer work in a hospital. Smith rushed into a burning house to rescue a child. These are all clear cases of unselfish behavior, and if the psychological egoist thinks that such cases do not occur, then he is just mistaken."

Such examples are obvious, and the thinkers who have been sympathetic to Psychological Egoism were certainly aware of them. Yet they have persisted in defending the view. Why? Partly it is because they have suspected that the "altruistic" explanations of behavior are too superficial—it *seems* that people are unselfish, but a deeper analysis of their motives might tell a different story. Perhaps Jones gives money for famine relief because his religion teaches that he will be rewarded in heaven. The man who works as a hospital volunteer may be driven by an inner need to atone for some past misdeed, or perhaps he simply enjoys this work, as other people enjoy playing chess. As for the woman who risks her life to save the child, we all know that such people are honored as heroes; perhaps she is motivated by a desire for public recognition. This technique of reinterpreting motives is perfectly general and may be repeated again and again. For any act of apparent altruism, a way can always be found to eliminate the altruism in favor of some more self-centered motive.

Thomas Hobbes (1588–1679) thought that Psychological

Egoism was probably true, but he was not satisfied with such a piecemeal approach. It is not theoretically elegant to deal with each action separately, "after the fact." If Psychological Egoism *is* true, we should be able to give a more general account of human motives, which would establish the theory once and for all. This is what Hobbes attempted to do. His method was to list the possible human motives, concentrating especially on the "altruistic" ones, and show how each could be understood in egoistic terms. Once this project was completed, he would have systematically eliminated altruism from our understanding of human nature. Here are two examples of Hobbes at work:

1. *Charity.* This is the most general motive that we ascribe to people when we think they are acting from a concern for others. *The Oxford English Dictionary* devotes almost four columns to "charity." It is defined variously as "The Christian love of our fellowman" and "Benevolence to one's neighbors." But for the psychological egoist, such neighborly love does not exist, and so charity must be understood in a radically different way. In his essay "On Human Nature," Hobbes describes it like this:

> There can be no greater argument to a man, of his own power, than to find himself able not only to accomplish his own desires, but also to assist other men in theirs: and this is that conception wherein consisteth *charity*.

Thus charity is a delight one takes in the demonstration of one's powers. The charitable man is demonstrating to himself, and to the world, that he is more capable than others. He can not only take care of himself, he has enough left over for others who are not so able as he. He is really just showing off his own superiority.

Of course Hobbes was aware that the charitable man may not *believe* that this is what he is doing. But we are not the best judges of our own motivations. It is only natural that we would interpret our actions in a way that is flattering to us (that is no more than the psychological egoist would expect!), and it is flattering to think that we are "unselfish." Hobbes's account aims to provide the *real* explanation of why we act as we do, not the superficial flattering account that we naturally want to believe.

2. *Pity.* What is it to pity other persons? We might think it is to sympathize with them, to feel unhappy about their misfortunes. And acting from this sympathy, we might try to help them. Hobbes thinks this is all right, as far as it goes, but it does not go far enough. The *reason* we are disturbed by other people's misfortunes is that we are reminded that the same thing might happen to us! "Pity," he says, "is imagination or fiction of future calamity to ourselves, proceeding from the sense of another man's calamity."

This account of pity turns out to be more powerful, from a theoretical point of view, than it first appears. It can explain very neatly some peculiar facts about the phenomenon. For example, it can explain why we feel greater pity when a good person suffers than when an evil person suffers. Pity, on Hobbes's account, requires a sense of identification with the person suffering—I pity you when I imagine *myself* in your place. But because each of us thinks of himself or herself as a good person, we do not identify very closely with those we think bad. Therefore, we do not pity the wicked in the same way we pity the good—our feelings of pity vary directly with the virtue of the person suffering, because our sense of identification varies in that way.

The strategy of reinterpreting motives is a persuasive method of reasoning; it has made a great many people feel that Psychological Egoism might be true. It especially appeals to a certain cynicism in us, a suspicion that people are not nearly as noble as they seem. But it is not a conclusive method of reasoning, for it cannot *prove* that Psychological Egoism is correct. The trouble is, it only shows that it is *possible* to interpret motives egoistically; it does nothing to show that the egoistic motives are deeper or truer than the altruistic explanations they are intended to replace. At most, the strategy shows that Psychological Egoism is possible. We still need other arguments to show it is true.

5.3. Two Arguments in Favor of Psychological Egoism

Two general arguments have often been advanced in favor of Psychological Egoism. They are "general" arguments, in the sense that each one seeks to establish at a stroke that *all* actions, and not merely some limited class of them, are motivated by self-interest. As will be seen, neither argument stands up very well under scrutiny.

1. The first argument goes as follows. If we describe one person's action as selfish and another person's action as unselfish, we are overlooking the crucial fact that in both cases, assuming the action is done voluntarily, *the person is merely doing what he most wants to do*. If Jones gives his money for the cause of famine relief rather than spending it on the movies, that only shows that he wanted to contribute to that cause more than he wanted to go to the movies—and why should he be praised for "unselfishness" when he is only doing what *he* most wants to do? His action is being dictated by his own desires, his own sense of what *he* wants most. Thus he cannot be said to be acting unselfishly. And since exactly the same may be said about *any* alleged act of altruism, we can conclude that Psychological Egoism must be true.

This argument has two primary flaws. First, it rests on the premise that people never voluntarily do anything except what they want to do. But this is plainly false; there are at least two kinds of actions that are exceptions to this generalization. One is actions that we may not want to do but that we do anyway as a means to an end that we want to achieve—for example, going to the dentist to stop a toothache. Such cases may, however, be regarded as consistent with the spirit of the argument, because the ends mentioned (such as stopping the toothache) are wanted.

Still, there are also actions that we do not because we want to nor even because they are means to an end we want to achieve, but because we feel that we *ought* to do them. For example, someone may do something because she has promised to do it, and thus feels obligated, even though she does not want to do it. It is sometimes suggested that in such cases we do the action because, after all, we want to keep our promises; so even here we are doing what we want. However, this will not work. If I have promised to do something and I do not want to do it, then it is simply false to say that I want to keep my promise. In such cases we feel a conflict precisely because we do *not* want to do what we feel obligated to do. If our desires and our sense of obligation *were* always in harmony, it would be a happier world. Unfortunately, we enjoy no such happy situation. It is an all too common experience to be pulled in different directions by desire and obligation. Jones's predicament may be like this: he *wants* to go to the movies, but he feels he *should* give the money for famine relief instead. Thus if he chooses to contribute the money, he is not simply doing what he wants to do. If he did that, he would go to the movies.

The argument has a second flaw. Suppose we were to concede, for the sake of argument, that all voluntary action is motivated by desire, or at least that Jones is so motivated. Even if this were granted, it would not follow that Jones is acting selfishly or from self-interest. For if Jones wants to do something to help starving people, even when it means forgoing his own enjoyments, that is precisely what makes him *un*-selfish. What else could unselfishness be, if not wanting to help others, even at some sacrifice to oneself? Another way to put the point is to say that it is the *object* of a want that determines whether it is selfish or not. The mere fact that I am acting on *my* wants does not mean that I am acting selfishly; it depends on *what it is* that I want. If I want only my own good and care nothing for others, then I am selfish; but if I also want other people to be happy and I act on *that* desire, then my action is not selfish.

Therefore, this argument goes wrong in just about every way that an argument can go wrong: the premises are not true, and even if they were true, the conclusion would not follow from them.

2. The second general argument for Psychological Egoism appeals to the fact that so-called unselfish actions produce a sense of self-satisfaction in the person who does them. Acting "unselfishly" makes people *feel good* about themselves. This has often been noted and has been put in various ways: "It gives him a clear conscience" or "He couldn't sleep at night if he had done otherwise" or "He would have been ashamed of himself for not doing it" are familiar ways of making the same point. This sense of self-satisfaction is a pleasant state of consciousness, which we desire and seek. Therefore, actions are "unselfish" only at a superficial level of analysis. If we dig deeper, we find that the *point* of acting "unselfishly" is really to

achieve this pleasant state of consciousness. Jones will feel much better about himself for having given the money for famine relief—if he had gone to the movies, he would have felt terrible about it—and that is the real point of the action.

According to a well-known story, this argument was once advanced by Abraham Lincoln. A nineteenth-century newspaper reported that

> Mr. Lincoln once remarked to a fellow-passenger on an old-time mud coach that all men were prompted by selfishness in doing good. His fellow-passenger was antagonizing this position when they were passing over a corduroy bridge that spanned a slough. As they crossed this bridge they espied an old razor-backed sow on the bank making a terrible noise because her pigs had got into the slough and were in danger of drowning. As the old coach began to climb the hill, Mr. Lincoln called out, "Driver, can't you stop just a moment?" Then Mr. Lincoln jumped out, ran back, and lifted the little pigs out of the mud and water and placed them on the bank. When he returned, his companion remarked: "Now, Abe, where does selfishness come in on this little episode?" "Why, bless your soul, Ed, that was the very essence of selfishness. I should have had no peace of mind all day had I gone on and left that suffering old sow worrying over those pigs. I did it to get peace of mind, don't you see?"

Lincoln was a better president than philosopher. His argument is vulnerable to the same sorts of objections as the previous one. Why should we think, merely because someone derives satisfaction from helping others, that this makes him selfish? Isn't the unselfish person precisely the one who *does* derive satisfaction from helping others, whereas the selfish person does not? If Lincoln "got peace of mind" from rescuing the piglets, does this show him to be selfish or, on the contrary, doesn't it show him to be compassionate and good-hearted? (If a person were truly selfish, why should it bother his conscience that others suffer—much less pigs?) Similarly, it is nothing more than sophistry to say, because Jones finds satisfaction in giving for famine relief, that he is selfish. If we say this rapidly, while thinking about something else, perhaps it will sound all right; but if we speak slowly and pay attention to what we are saying, it sounds plain silly.

Moreover, suppose we ask *why* Jones derives satisfaction from contributing for famine relief. The answer is, it is because Jones is the kind of person who cares about other people: even if they are strangers to him, he doesn't want them to go hungry, and he is willing to take action to help them. If Jones were not this kind of person, then he would take no special pleasure in assisting them; and as we have already seen, this is the mark of unselfishness, not selfishness.

There is a general lesson to be learned here, having to do with the nature of desire and its objects. If we have a positive attitude toward the attainment of some goal, then we may derive satisfaction from attaining it. But the *object* of our attitude is *the attainment of that goal;* and we must want to attain the goal *before* we can find any satisfaction in it. We do not first desire some sort of "pleasurable consciousness" and then try to figure out how to achieve it. Rather, we desire all sorts of different things—money, a new car, to be a better chess player, to get a promotion in our work, and so on—and because we desire these things, we derive satisfaction from getting them. And so if someone desires the welfare and happiness of other people, he will derive satisfaction from helping them; but this does not mean that those good feelings are the *object* of his desire. *They* are not what he is after. Nor does it mean that he is in any way selfish on account of having those feelings.

These two arguments are the ones most commonly advanced in defense of Psychological Egoism. It is a measure of the weakness of the theory that stronger arguments have not been forthcoming.

5.4. Clearing Away Some Confusions

One of the most powerful theoretical motives is a desire for simplicity. When we set out to explain something, we would like to find as *simple* an explanation as possible. This is certainly true in the sciences—the simpler a scientific theory, the greater its appeal. Consider phenomena as diverse as planetary motion, the tides, and the way objects fall to the surface of the earth when released from a height. These appear, at first, to be very different; it would seem that we would need a multitude of different principles to explain them all. Who would suspect that they could all be explained by a single simple principle? Yet the theory of gravity does just that. The theory's ability to bring diverse phenomena together under a single explanatory principle is one of its great virtues. It makes order out of chaos.

In the same way, when we think about human conduct, we would like to find one principle that explains it all. We want a single simple formula, if we can find one, that would unite the diverse phenomena of human behavior, in the way that simple formulas in physics bring together apparently diverse phenomena. Since it is obvious that self-regard is an overwhelmingly important factor in motivation, it is only natural to wonder whether all motivation might not be explained in terms of it. And so the idea of Psychological Egoism is born.

But, most philosophers and psychologists would agree today, it is stillborn. The fundamental idea behind Psychological Egoism cannot even be expressed without falling into confusion; and once these confusions have been cleared away, the theory no longer seems even plausible.

The first confusion is between selfishness and self-interest. When we think about it, the two are clearly not the same. If I see a physician because I am feeling poorly, I am acting in my own self-interest, but no one would think of calling me "selfish" on account of it. Similarly, brushing my teeth, working hard at my job, and obeying the law are all in my self-interest, but none of these are examples of selfish conduct. This is because selfish behavior is behavior that ignores the interests of others, in circumstances in which their interests ought not to be ignored. The concept of "selfishness" has a definite evaluative flavor; to call people selfish is not just to describe their action but to criticize it. Thus you would not be called selfish for eating a normal meal in normal circumstances (although this would surely be in your self-interest); but you would be called selfish for hoarding food while others are starving.

A second confusion is between self-interested behavior and the pursuit of pleasure. We do lots of things because we enjoy them, but that does not mean we are acting from self-interest. The man who continues to smoke cigarettes even after learning about the connection between smoking and cancer is surely not acting from self-interest, not even by his own standards—self-interest would dictate that he quit smoking at once—and he is not acting altruistically either. He *is*, no doubt, smoking for the pleasure of it, but this only shows that undisciplined pleasure seeking and acting from self-interest are very different. This is what led Joseph Butler, the leading eighteenth-century critic of egoism, to remark, "The thing to be lamented is, not that men have so great regard to their own good or interest in the present world, for they have not enough."

Taken together, the last two paragraphs show (a) that it is false that all actions are selfish and (b) that it is false that all actions are done from self-interest. When we brush our teeth, at least in normal circumstances, we are not acting selfishly; therefore not all actions are selfish. And when we smoke cigarettes, we are not acting out of self-interest; therefore not all actions are done from self-interest. It is worth noting that these two points do not depend on examples of altruism; even if there were no such thing as altruistic behavior, Psychological Egoism would, according to these arguments, *still* be false!

A third confusion is the common but false assumption that a concern for one's own welfare is incompatible with any genuine concern for others. Since it is obvious that everyone (or very nearly everyone) does desire his or her own well-being, it might be thought that no one can really be concerned for the well-being of others. But again, this is surely a false dichotomy. There is no inconsistency in desiring that everyone, including oneself *and* others, be happy. To be sure, it may happen on occasion that our interests conflict with the interests of others, in the sense that both cannot be satisfied. In these cases we have to make hard choices. But even in these cases we sometimes opt for the interests of others, especially when the others are our friends and family. But more important, not all cases are like this. Sometimes we are able to promote the welfare of others when our own interests are not involved at all. In those circumstances, not even the strongest self-regard need prevent us from acting considerately toward others.

Once these confusions are cleared away, there seems little reason to think Psychological Egoism is a plausible theory. On the contrary, it seems decidedly implausible. If we simply observe people's behavior with an open mind, we find that much of it is motivated by self-regard, but by no means all of it. There may indeed be one simple formula, as yet undiscovered, that would explain all of human behavior—but Psychological Egoism is not it.

5.5. The Deepest Error in Psychological Egoism

The preceding discussion may seem relentlessly negative—even objectionably so. "If Psychological Egoism is so obviously confused," you may ask, "and if there are no plausible arguments in its favor, why have so many intelligent people been attracted to it?" It is a fair question. Part of the answer, I think, is the almost irresistible urge toward theoretical simplicity; another part is the attraction of what appears to be a hard-headed, deflationary attitude toward human pretensions. But there is a deeper reason: Psychological Egoism was accepted by many thinkers because it appeared to them to be *irrefutable*. And in a certain sense, they were right. Yet in another sense, the theory's immunity from refutation is its deepest flaw.

To explain, let me first tell a (true) story that might appear to be far from our subject.

A few years ago a group of investigators led by Dr. David Rosenham, professor of psychology and law at Stanford University, had themselves admitted as patients to various mental institutions. The hospital staffs did not know there was anything special about them; the investigators were thought to be simply patients. The investigators' purpose was to see how they would be treated.

The investigators were perfectly "sane," whatever that means, but their very presence in the hospitals created the assumption that they were mentally disturbed. Although they behaved normally—they did nothing to feign illness—they soon discovered that everything they did was interpreted as a sign of some sort of mental problem. When some of them were found to be taking notes on their experiences, entries were made in their records such as "patient engages in writing behavior." During one interview, one "patient" confessed that although he was closer to his mother as a small child, he became more attached to his father as he grew older—a perfectly normal turn of events. But this was taken as evidence of "unstable relationships in childhood." Even their protestations of normalcy were turned against them. One of the real patients warned them: "Never tell a doctor that you're well. He won't believe you. That's called a 'flight into health.' Tell him you're still sick, but you're feeling a lot better. That's called insight."

No one on the hospital staffs ever caught on to the hoax. The real patients, however, did see through it. One of them told an investigator, "You're not crazy. You're checking up on the hospital." And so he was.

What the investigators learned was that *once a hypothesis is accepted, everything may be interpreted to support it*. The hypothesis was that the pseudopatients were mentally disturbed; once that became the controlling assumption, it did not matter how they behaved. Everything they did would be construed so as to fit the assumption. But the "success" of this technique of interpretation did not prove the hypothesis was true. If anything, it was a sign that something had gone wrong.

The hypothesis that the pseudopatients were disturbed was faulty because, at least for the hospital staffs, it was *untestable*. If a hypothesis purports to say something about the world, then there must be some conditions that could verify it and some that conceivably could refute it. Otherwise, it is meaningless. Consider this example: suppose someone says "Kareem Abdul-Jabbar cannot get into my Volkswagen." We know perfectly well what this means, because we can imagine the circumstances that would make it true and the circumstances that would make it false: to test the statement, we take the car to Kareem, invite him to step inside, and see what happens. If it turns out one way, the statement is true; if it turns out the other way, the statement is false. The problem with the hypothesis about the pseudopatients' mental health, as it was applied within the hospital setting, was that nothing could have refuted it. Such hypotheses may be immune from refutation, but their immunity is purchased at too dear a price— they no longer say anything significant about the world.

Psychological Egoism is involved in this same error. All our experience tells us that people act from a great variety of motives: greed, anger, lust, love, and hate, to name only a few. Sometimes, people think only of themselves. At other times, they do not think of themselves at all and act from a concern for others. The common distinction between self-regard and unselfishness gets its meaning from this contrast. But then Psychological Egoism tells us that there is *really* only one motive, self-regard, and this seems a new and fascinating revelation. We must have been wrong. But as the theory unfolds, it turns out that we were not wrong at all. The psychological egoist does not deny that people act in the variety of ways they have always appeared to act in. In the ordinary sense of the term, people are still, sometimes, unselfish. In effect, the psychological egoist has only announced his determination to *interpret* people's behavior in a certain way, *no matter what they do*. Therefore, *nothing that anyone could do could possibly count as evidence against the hypothesis*. The thesis is irrefutable, but for that very reason it turns out to have no factual content. It is not a new and fascinating revelation at all.

I am not saying that the hypothesis of the pseudopatients' mental illness or the hypothesis of Psychological Egoism are meaningless in themselves. The trouble is not so much with the hypotheses as with the people who manipulate the facts to fit them. The staffs of the mental institutions, and the estimable Hobbes, *could* have allowed some facts to count as falsifying their assumptions. Then, their hypotheses would have been meaningful but would have been seen to be plainly false. That is the risk one must take. Paradoxically, if we do not allow some way in which we might be mistaken, we lose all chance of being right.

CHAPTER 6

*E*thical Egoism

The achievement of his own happiness is man's highest moral purpose.

AYN RAND, *THE VIRTUE OF SELFISHNESS* (1961)

6.1. Is There a Duty to Contribute for Famine Relief?

Each year millions of people die of malnutrition and related health problems. A common pattern among children in poor countries is death from dehydration caused by diarrhea brought on by malnutrition. The executive director of the United Nations Children's Fund (UNICEF) has estimated that about 15,000 children die in this way *every day*. That comes to 5,475,000 children annually. Even if his estimate is too high, the number that die is staggering.

For those of us in the affluent countries, this poses an acute moral problem. We spend money on ourselves, not only for the necessities of life but for innumerable luxuries—for fine automobiles, fancy clothes, stereos, sports, movies, and so on. In our country, even people with modest incomes enjoy such things. The problem is that we *could* forgo our luxuries and give the money for famine relief instead. The fact that we don't suggest that we regard our luxuries as more important than feeding the hungry.

Why do we allow people to starve to death when we could save them? Very few of us actually believe our luxuries are that important. Most of us, if asked the question directly, would probably be a bit embarrassed, and we would say that we probably should do more for famine relief. The explanation of why we do not is, at least in part, that we hardly ever think of the problem. Living our own comfortable lives, we are effectively insulated from it. The starving people are dying at some distance from us; we do not see them and we can avoid even thinking of them. When we do think of them, it is only abstractly, as bloodless statistics. Unfortunately for the starving, statistics do not have much power to motivate action.

But leaving aside the question of *why* we behave as we do, what is our *duty?* What *should* we do? We might think of this as the "common-sense" view of the matter: morality requires that we balance our own interests against the interests of others. It is understandable, of course, that we look out for our own interests, and no one can be faulted for attending to his own basic needs. But at the same time the needs of others are also important, and when we can help others—especially at little cost to ourselves—we should do so. Suppose you are thinking of spending ten dollars on a trip to the movies, when you are reminded that ten dollars could buy food for a starving child. Thus you could do a great service for the child at little cost to yourself. Common-sense morality would say, then, that you should give the money for famine relief rather than spending it on the movies.

This way of thinking involves a general assumption about our moral duties: it is assumed that we have moral duties *to other people*—and not merely duties that we create, such as by making a promise or incurring a debt. We have "natural" duties to others *simply because they are people who could be helped or harmed by our actions.* If a certain action would benefit (or harm) other people, then that is a reason why we should (or should not) do that action. The common-sense assumption is that other people's interests *count,* for their own sakes, from a moral point of view.

But one person's common sense is another person's naive platitude. Some thinkers have maintained that, in fact, we have no "natural" duties to other people. *Ethical Egoism* is the idea that each person ought to pursue his or her own self-interest exclusively. It is different from Psychological Egoism, which is a theory of human nature concerned with how people *do* behave—Psychological Egoism says that people do in fact always pursue their own interests. Ethical Egoism, by contrast, is a normative theory—that is, a theory about how we *ought* to behave. Regardless of how we do behave, Ethical Egoism says we have no moral duty except to do what is best for ourselves.

It is a challenging theory. It contradicts some of our deepest moral beliefs—beliefs held by most of us, at any rate—but it is not easy to refute. We will examine the most important arguments for and against it. If it turns out to be true, then of course that is immensely important. But even if it turns out to be false, there is still much to be learned from examining it—we may, for example, gain some insight into the reasons why we *do* have obligations to other people.

But before looking at the arguments, we should be a little clearer about exactly what this theory says and what it does not say. In the first place, Ethical Egoism does not say that one should promote one's own interests *as well as* the interests of others. That would be an ordinary, unexceptional view. Ethical Egoism is the radical view that one's *only* duty is to promote one's own interests. According to Ethical Egoism, there is only one ultimate principle of conduct, the principle of self-interest, and this principle sums up *all* of one's natural duties and obligations.

However, Ethical Egoism does not say that you should *avoid* actions that help others, either. It may very well be that in many instances your interests coincide with the interests of others, so that in helping yourself you will be aiding others willy-nilly. Or it may happen that aiding others is an effective *means* for creating some benefit for yourself. Ethical Egoism does not forbid such actions; in fact, it may demand them. The theory insists only that in such cases the benefit to others is not what makes the act right. What makes the act right is, rather, the fact that it is to one's own advantage.

Finally, Ethical Egoism does not imply that in pursuing one's interests one ought always to do what one wants to do, or what gives one the most pleasure in the short run. Someone may want to do something that is not good for himself or that will eventually cause himself more grief than pleasure— he may want to drink a lot or smoke cigarettes or take drugs or waste his best years at the race track. Ethical Egoism would frown on all this, regardless of the momentary pleasure it affords. It says that a person ought to do what *really is* to his or her own best advantage, *over the long run*. It endorses selfishness, but it doesn't endorse foolishness.

6.2. Three Arguments in Favor of Ethical Egoism

What reasons can be advanced to support this doctrine? Why should anyone think it is true? Unfortunately, the theory is asserted more often than it is argued for. Many of its supporters apparently think its truth is self-evident, so that arguments are not needed. When it *is* argued for, three lines of reasoning are most commonly used.

1. The first argument has several variations, each suggesting the same general point:

a. Each of us is intimately familiar with our own individual wants and needs. Moreover, each of us is uniquely placed to pursue those wants and needs effectively. At the same time, we know the desires and needs of other people only imperfectly, and we are not well situated to pursue them. Therefore, it is reasonable to believe that if we set out to be "our brother's keeper," we would often bungle the job and end up doing more mischief than good.

b. At the same time, the policy of "looking out for others" is an offensive intrusion into other people's privacy; it is essentially a policy of minding other people's business.

c. Making other people the object of one's "charity" is degrading to them; it robs them of their individual dignity and self-respect. The offer of charity says, in effect, that they are not competent to care for themselves; and the statement is self-fulfilling—they cease to be self-reliant and become passively dependent on others. That is why the recipients of "charity" are so often resentful rather than appreciative.

What this adds up to is that the policy of "looking out for others" is self-defeating. If we want to promote the best interests of everyone alike, we should *not* adopt so-called altruistic policies of behavior. On the contrary, if each person looks after his or her *own* interests, it is more likely that everyone will be better off, in terms of both physical and emotional well-being. Thus Robert G. Olson says in his book *The Morality of Self-Interest* (1965), "The individual is most likely to contribute to social betterment by rationally pursuing his own best long-range interests." Or as Alexander Pope said more poetically,

> Thus God and nature formed the general frame
> And bade self-love and social be the same.

It is possible to quarrel with this argument on a number of grounds. Of course no one favors bungling, butting in, or depriving people of their self-respect. But is this really what we are doing when we feed hungry children? Is the starving child in Ethiopia really harmed when we "intrude" into "her business" by supplying food? It hardly seems likely. Yet we can set this point aside, for considered as an argument for Ethical Egoism, this way of thinking has an even more serious defect.

The trouble is that it isn't really an argument *for Ethical Egoism* at all. The argument concludes that we should adopt certain policies of action; and on the surface they appear to be egoistic policies. However, the *reason* it is said we should adopt those policies is decidedly *unegoistic*. The reason is one that to an egoist shouldn't matter. It is said that we should adopt those policies because doing so will promote the "betterment of society"—but according to Ethical Egoism, that is something we should not be concerned about. Spelled out fully, with everything laid on the table, the argument says:

(1) We ought to do whatever will promote the best interests of everyone alike.

(2) The interests of everyone will best be promoted if each of us adopts the policy of pursuing our own interests exclusively.

(3) Therefore, each of us should adopt the policy of pursuing our own interests exclusively.

If we accept this reasoning, then we are not ethical egoists at all. Even though we might end up *behaving* like egoists, our ultimate principle is one of beneficence—we are doing what we think will help everyone, not merely what we think will benefit ourselves. Rather than being egoists, we turn out to be altruists with a peculiar view of what in fact promotes the general welfare.

2. The second argument was put forward with some force by Ayn Rand, a writer little heeded by professional philosophers but who nevertheless was enormously popular on college campuses during the 1960s and 1970s. Ethical Egoism, in her view, is the only ethical philosophy that respects the integrity of the individual human life. She regarded the ethics of "altruism" as a totally destructive idea, both in society as a whole and in the lives of individuals taken in by it. Altruism, to her way of thinking, leads to a denial of the value of the individual. It says to a person: *your* life is merely something that may be sacrificed. "If a man accepts the ethics of altruism," she writes, "his first concern is not how to live his life, but how to sacrifice it." Moreover, those who would *promote* this idea are beneath contempt—they are parasites who, rather than working to build and sustain their own lives, leech off those who do. Again, she writes:

> Parasites, moochers, looters, brutes and thugs can be of no value to a human being—nor can he gain any benefit from living in a society geared to *their* needs, demands and protections, a society that treats him as a sacrificial animal and penalizes him for his virtues in order to reward *them* for their vices, which means: a society based on the ethics of altruism.

By "sacrificing one's life" Rand does not necessarily mean anything so dramatic as dying. A person's life consists (in part) of projects undertaken and goods earned and created. To demand that a person abandon his projects or give up his goods is also a clear effort to "sacrifice his life." Furthermore, throughout her writings Rand also suggests that there is a *metaphysical* basis for egoistic ethics. Somehow, it is the only ethics that takes seriously the *reality* of the individual person. She bemoans "the enormity of the extent to which altruism erodes men's capacity to grasp . . . the value of an individual life; it reveals a mind from which the reality of a human being has been wiped out."

What, then, of the starving people? It might be argued, in response, that Ethical Egoism "reveals a mind from which the reality of a human being has been wiped out"—namely, the human being who is starving. Rand quotes with approval the evasive answer given by one of her followers: "Once, when Barbara Brandon was asked by a student: 'What will happen to the poor . . . ?'—she answered: 'If *you* want to help them, you will not be stopped.'"

All these remarks are, I think, part of one continuous argument that can be summarized like this:

(1) A person has only one life to live. If we place any value on the individual—that is, if the individual has any moral worth—then we must agree that this life is of supreme importance. After all, it is all one has, and all one is.

(2) The ethics of altruism regards the life of the individual as something one must be ready to sacrifice for the good of others.

(3) Therefore, the ethics of altruism does not take seriously the value of the human individual.

(4) Ethical Egoism, which allows each person to view his or her own life as being of ultimate value, *does* take the human individual seriously—in fact, it is the only philosophy that does so.

(5) Thus, Ethical Egoism is the philosophy that ought to be accepted.

The problem with this argument, as you may already have noticed, is that it relies on picturing the alternatives in such an extreme way. "The ethics of altruism" is taken to be such an extreme philosophy that *nobody*, with the possible exception of certain monks, would find it congenial. As Ayn Rand presents it, altruism implies that one's own interests have *no* value, and that *any* demand by others calls for sacrificing them. If that is the alternative, then any other view, including Ethical Egoism, will look good by comparison. But this is hardly a fair picture of the choices. What we called the common-sense view stands somewhere between the two extremes. It says that one's own interests and the interests of others are both important and must be balanced against one another. Sometimes, when the balancing is done, it will turn out that one should act in the interests of others; other times, it will turn out that one should take care of oneself. So even if the Randian argument refutes the extreme "ethics of altruism," it does not follow that one must accept the other extreme of Ethical Egoism.

3. The third line of reasoning takes a somewhat different approach. Ethical Egoism is usually presented as a *revisionist* moral philosophy, that is, as a philosophy that says our common-sense moral views are mistaken and need to be changed. It is possible, however, to interpret Ethical Egoism in a much less radical way, as a theory that *accepts* common-sense morality and offers a surprising account of its basis.

The less radical interpretation goes as follows. In everyday life, we assume that we are obliged to obey certain rules. We must avoid doing harm to others, speak the truth, keep our promises, and so on. At first glance, these duties appear to be very different from one another. They appear to have little in common. Yet from a theoretical point of view, we may wonder whether there is not some hidden *unity* underlying the hodgepodge of separate duties. Perhaps there is some small number of fundamental principles that explain all the rest, just as in physics there are basic principles that bring together and explain diverse phenomena. From a theoretical point of view, the smaller the number of basic principles, the better. Best of all would be *one* fundamental principle, from which all the rest could be derived. Ethical Egoism, then, would be the theory that all our duties are ultimately derived from the one fundamental principle of self-interest.

Taken in this way, Ethical Egoism is not such a radical doctrine. It does not challenge common-sense morality; it only tries to explain and systematize it. And it does a surprisingly successful job. It can provide plausible explanations of the duties mentioned above, and more:

a. If we make a habit of doing things that are harmful to other people, people will not be reluctant to do things that will harm *us*. We will be shunned and despised; others will not have us as friends and will not do us favors when we need them. If our offenses against others are serious enough, we may even up in jail. Thus it is to our own advantage to avoid harming others.

b. If we lie to other people, we will suffer all the ill effects of a bad reputation. People will distrust us and avoid doing business with us. We will often need for people to be honest with us, but we can hardly expect them to feel much of an obligation to be honest with us if they know we have not been honest with them. Thus it is to our own advantage to be truthful.

c. It is to our own advantage to be able to enter into mutually beneficial arrangements with other people. To benefit from those arrangements, we need to be able to rely on others to keep their parts of the bargains we make with them—we need to be able to rely on them to keep their promises to us. But we can hardly expect others to keep their promises to us if we are not willing to keep our promises to them. Therefore, from the point of view of self-interest, we should keep our promises.

Pursuing this line of reasoning, Thomas Hobbes suggested that the principle of Ethical Egoism leads to nothing less than the Golden Rule: we should "do unto others" *because* if we do, others will be more likely to "do unto us."

Does this argument succeed in establishing Ethical Egoism as a viable theory of morality? It is, in my opinion at least, the best try. But there are two serious objections to it. In the first place, the argument does not prove quite as much as it needs to prove. At best, it shows only that *as a general rule* it is to one's own advantage to avoid harming others. It does not show that this is *always* so. And it could not show that, for even though it may usually be to one's advantage to avoid harming others, sometimes it is not. Sometimes one might even *gain* from treating another person badly. In that case, the obligation not to harm the other person could *not* be derived from the principle of Ethical Egoism. Thus it appears that not all our moral obligations can be explained as derivable from self-interest.

But set that point aside. There is still a more fundamental question to be asked about the proposed theory. Suppose it is true that, say, contributing money for famine relief is somehow to one's own advantage. It does not follow that this is the only reason, or even the most basic reason, why doing so is a morally good thing. (For example, the most basic reason might be *in order to help the starving people.* The fact that doing so is also to one's own advantage might be only a secondary, less important, consideration.) A demonstration that one could *derive* this duty from self-interest does not prove that self-interest is the *only reason* one has this duty. Only if you accept an additional proposition—namely, the proposition that there is no reason for giving *other than* self-interest—will you find Ethical Egoism a plausible theory.

6.3. Three Arguments Against Ethical Egoism

Ethical Egoism has haunted twentieth-century moral philosophy. It has not been a popular doctrine; the most important philosophers have rejected it outright. But it has never been very far from their minds. Although no thinker of consequence has defended it, almost everyone has felt it necessary to explain why he was rejecting it—as though the very possibility that it might be correct was hanging in the air, threatening to smother their other ideas. As the merits of the various "refutations" have been debated, philosophers have returned to it again and again.

The following three arguments are typical of the refutations proposed by contemporary philosophers.

1. In his book *The Moral Point of View* (1958), Kurt Baier argues that Ethical Egoism cannot be correct because it cannot provide solutions for conflicts of interest. We need moral rules, he says, only because our interests sometimes come into conflict. (If they never conflicted, then there would be no problems to solve and hence no need for the kind of guidance that morality provides.) But Ethical Egoism does not help to resolve conflicts of interest; it only exacerbates them. Baier argues for this by introducing a fanciful example:

> Let B and K be candidates for the presidency of a certain country and let it be granted that it is in the interest of either to be elected, but that only one can succeed. It would then be in the interest of B but against the interest of K if B were elected, and vice versa, and therefore in the interest of B but against the interest of K if K were liq-

uidated, and vice versa. But from this it would follow that B ought to liquidate K, that it is wrong for B not to do so, that B has not "done his duty" until he has liquidated K; and vice versa. Similarly K, knowing that his own liquidation is in the interest of B and therefore, anticipating B's attempts to secure it, ought to take steps to foil B's endeavors. It would be wrong for him not to do so. He would "not have done his duty" until he had made sure of stopping B. . . .

This is obviously absurd. For morality is designed to apply in just such cases, namely, those where interests conflict. But if the point of view of morality were that of self-interest, then there could never be moral solutions of conflicts of interest.

Does this argument prove that Ethical Egoism is unacceptable? It does, *if* the conception of morality to which it appeals is accepted. The argument assumes that an adequate morality must provide solutions for conflicts of interest in such a way that everyone concerned can live together harmoniously. The conflict between B and K, for example, should be resolved so that they would no longer be at odds with one another. (One would not then have a duty to do something that the other has a duty to prevent.) Ethical Egoism does not do that, and if you think an ethical theory should, then you will not find Ethical Egoism acceptable.

But a defender of Ethical Egoism might reply that *he* does not accept this conception of morality. For him, life is essentially a long series of conflicts in which each person is struggling to come out on top; and the principle he accepts—the principle of Ethical Egoism—simply urges each one to do his or her best to win. On his view, the moralist is not like a courtroom judge, who resolves disputes. Instead, he is like the Commissioner of Boxing, who urges each fighter to do his best. So the conflict between B and K will be "resolved" not by the application of an ethical theory but by one or the other of them winning the struggle. The egoist will not be embarrassed by this—on the contrary, he will think it no more than a realistic view of the nature of things.

2. Some philosophers, including Baier, have leveled an even more serious charge against Ethical Egoism. They have

argued that it is a *logically inconsistent* doctrine—that is, they say it leads to logical contradictions. If this is true, then Ethical Egoism is indeed a mistaken theory, for no theory can be true if it is self-contradictory.

Consider B and K again. As Baier explains their predicament, it is in B's interest to kill K, and obviously it is in K's interest to prevent it. But, Baier says,

> if K prevents B from liquidating him, his act must be said to be both wrong and not wrong—wrong because it is the prevention of what B ought to do, his duty, and wrong for B not to do it; not wrong because it is what K ought to do, his duty, and wrong for K not to do it. But one and the same act (logically) cannot be both morally wrong and not morally wrong.

Now, does *this* argument prove that Ethical Egoism is unacceptable? At first glance it seems persuasive. However, it is a complicated argument, so we need to set it out with each step individually identified. Then we will be in a better position to evaluate it. Spelled out fully, it looks like this:

(1) Suppose it is each person's duty to do what is in his own best interests.

(2) It is in B's best interest to liquidate K.

(3) It is in K's best interest to prevent B from liquidating him.

(4) Therefore B's duty is to liquidate K, and K's duty is to prevent B from doing it.

(5) But it is wrong to prevent someone from doing his duty.

(6) Therefore it is wrong for K to prevent B from liquidating him.

(7) Therefore it is both wrong and not wrong for K to prevent B from liquidating him.

(8) But no act can be both wrong and not wrong—that is a self-contradiction.

(9) Therefore the assumption with which we started—that it is each person's duty to do what is in his own best interests—cannot be true.

When the argument is set out in this way, we can see its hidden flaw. The logical contradiction—that it is both wrong and not wrong for K to prevent B from liquidating him—does *not* follow simply from the principle of Ethical Egoism. It follows from that principle *and* the additional premise expressed in step (5)—namely, that "it is wrong to prevent someone from doing his duty." Thus we are not compelled by the logic of the argument to reject Ethical Egoism. Instead, we could simply reject this additional premise, and the contradiction would be avoided. That is surely what the ethical egoist would want to do, for the ethical egoist would never say, without qualification, that it is always wrong to prevent someone from doing his duty. He would say, instead, that *whether one ought to prevent someone from doing his duty depends entirely on whether it would be to one's own advantage to do so.* Regardless of whether we think this is a correct view, it is, at the very least, a *consistent* view, and so this attempt to convict the egoist of self-contradiction fails.

3. Finally, we come to the argument that I think comes closest to an outright refutation of Ethical Egoism. It is also the most interesting of the arguments, because at the same time it provides the most insight into why the interests of other people *should* matter to a moral agent.

Before this argument is presented, we need to look briefly at a general point about moral values. So let us set Ethical Egoism aside for a moment and consider this related matter.

There is a whole family of moral views that have this in common: they all involve dividing people into groups and saying that the interests of some groups count for more than the interests of other groups. Racism is the most conspicuous example; it involves dividing people into groups according to race and assigning greater importance to the interests of one race than to others. The practical result is that members of the preferred race are to be *treated better* than the others. Anti-Semitism works the same way, and so can nationalism. People in the grip of such views will think, in effect: "*My* race counts for more," or "Those who believe in *my* religion count for more," or "*My* country counts for more," and so on.

Can such views be defended? Those who accept them are

usually not much interested in argument—racists, for example, rarely try to offer rational grounds for their position. But suppose they did. What could they say?

There is a general principle that stands in the way of any such defense, namely: *We can justify treating people differently only if we can show that there is some factual difference between them that is relevant to justifying the difference in treatment.* For example, if one person is admitted to law school while another is rejected, this can be justified by pointing out that the first graduated from college with honors and scored well on the admissions test, while the second dropped out of college and never took the test. However, if *both* graduated with honors and did well on the entrance examination—in other words, if they are in all relevant respects equally well qualified—then it is merely arbitrary to admit one but not the other.

Can a racist point to any differences between, say, white people and black people that would justify treating them differently? In the past, racists have sometimes attempted to do this by picturing blacks as stupid, lacking in ambition, and the like. *If* this were true, then it might justify treating them differently, in at least some circumstances. (This is the deep purpose of racist stereotypes—to provide the "relevant differences" needed to justify differences in treatment.) But of course it is not true, and in fact there are no such general differences between the races. Thus racism is an *arbitrary* doctrine, in that it advocates treating some people differently even though there are no differences between them to justify it.

Ethical Egoism is a moral theory of the same type. It advocates that each of us divides the world into two categories of people—ourselves and all the rest—and that we regard the interests of those in the first group as more important than the interests of those in the second group. But each of us can ask, what is the difference between myself and others that justifies placing myself in this special category? Am I more intelligent? Do I enjoy my life more? Are my accomplishments greater? Do I have needs or abilities that are so different from the needs or abilities of others? *What is it that makes me so special?* Failing an answer, it turns out that Ethical Egoism is an arbitrary doctrine, in the same way that racism is arbitrary.

The argument, then, is this:

(1) Any moral doctrine that assigns greater importance to the interests of one group than to those of another is unacceptably arbitrary unless there is some difference between the members of the groups that justifies treating them differently.

(2) Ethical Egoism would have each person assign greater importance to his or her own interests than to the interests of others. *But there is no general difference between oneself and others, to which each person can appeal, that justifies this difference in treatment.*

(3) Therefore, Ethical Egoism is unacceptably arbitrary.

And this, in addition to arguing against Ethical Egoism, also sheds some light on the question of why we should care about others.

We should care about the interests of other people *for the very same reason we care about our own interests;* for their needs and desires are comparable to our own. Consider, one last time, the starving people we could feed by giving up some of our luxuries. Why should we care about them? We care about ourselves, of course—if *we* were starving, we would go to almost any lengths to get food. But what is the difference between us and them? Does hunger affect them any less? Are they somehow less deserving than we? If we can find no relevant difference between us and them, then we must admit that if *our* needs should be met, so should *theirs*. It is this realization, that we are on a par with one another, that is the deepest reason why our morality must include some recognition of the needs of others, and why, then, Ethical Egoism fails as a moral theory.

CHAPTER 7

The Utilitarian Approach

Given our present perspective, it is amazing that Christian ethics down through the centuries could have accepted almost unanimously the sententious doctrine that "the end does not justify the means." We have to ask now, "If the end does not justify the means, what does?" The answer is, obviously, "Nothing!"

JOSEPH FLETCHER, *MORAL RESPONSIBILITY* (1967)

7.1. The Revolution in Ethics

Philosophers like to think that their ideas can change society. Often it is a vain hope: philosophers write books that are read, perhaps, by a few other like-minded thinkers, while the rest of the world goes on unaffected. On occasion, however, a philosophical theory can profoundly alter the way people think. Utilitarianism, a theory proposed by David Hume (1711–1776) but given definitive formulation by Jeremy Bentham (1748–1832) and John Stuart Mill (1806–1873), is a case in point.

The late eighteenth and nineteenth centuries witnessed an astonishing series of upheavals. The modern nation-state was emerging in the aftermath of the French Revolution and the wreckage of the Napoleonic empire; the revolutions of 1848 showed the continuing power of the new ideas of "liberty, equality, fraternity"; in America, a new country with a new kind of constitution was born, and its bloody civil war was to put an end, finally, to slavery in Western civilization; and all the while the industrial revolution was bringing about nothing less than a total restructuring of society.

It is not surprising that in the midst of all this change people might begin to think differently about ethics. The old values—the old ways of thinking—were very much up in the air, open to challenge. Against this background, Bentham's argument for a new conception of morality had a powerful influence. Morality, he urged, is not a matter of pleasing God, nor is it a matter of faithfulness to abstract rules. Morality is nothing more than the attempt to bring about as much happiness as possible in this world.

Bentham argued that there is one ultimate moral principle, namely "the Principle of Utility." This principle requires that whenever we have a choice between alternative actions or social policies, we must choose the one that has the best overall consequences for everyone concerned. Or, as he put it in his book *The Principles of Morals and Legislation,* published in the year of the French Revolution:

> By the Principle of Utility is meant that principle which approves or disapproves of every action whatsoever, according to the tendency which it appears to have to augment or diminish the happiness of the party whose interest is in question; or what is the same thing in other words, to promote or to oppose that happiness.

Bentham was the leader of a group of philosophical radicals whose aim was to reform the laws and institutions of England along utilitarian lines. One of his followers was James Mill, the distinguished Scottish philosopher, historian, and economist. James Mill's son, John Stuart Mill, would become the leading advocate of utilitarian moral theory for the next generation, and so the Benthamite movement would continue unabated even after its founder's death.

Bentham was fortunate to have such disciples. John Stuart Mill's advocacy was, if anything, even more elegant and persuasive than the master's. In his *Utilitarianism* (1861), Mill presents the main idea of the theory in the following way. First, we envision a certain state of affairs that we would like see come about—a state of affairs in which all people are as happy as they can be:

> According to the Greatest Happiness Principle . . . the ultimate end, with reference to and for the sake of which all other things are desirable (whether we are consider-

ing our own good or that of other people), is an existence exempt as far as possible from pain, and as rich as possible in enjoyments.

The primary rule of morality can, then, be stated quite simply. It is to act so as to bring about this state of affairs, insofar as that is possible:

> This, being, according to the utilitarian opinion, the end of human action, is necessarily also the standard of morality, which may accordingly be defined, as the rules and precepts for human conduct, by the observance of which an existence such as has been described might be, to the greatest extent possible, secured to all mankind, and not to them only, but, so far as the nature of things admits, to the whole of sentient creation.

In deciding what to do, we should, therefore, ask what course of conduct would promote the greatest amount of happiness for all those who will be affected. Morality requires that we do what is best from that point of view.

At first glance, this may not seem like such a radical idea—in fact it may seem a mild truism. Who could argue with the proposition that we should oppose suffering and promote happiness? Yet in their own way Bentham and Mill were leading a revolution as radical as either of the other two great intellectual revolutions in the nineteenth century, those of Marx and Darwin. To understand the radicalness of the Principle of Utility, we have to appreciate what it *leaves out* of its picture of morality: gone are all references to God or to abstract moral rules "written in the heavens." Morality is no longer to be understood as faithfulness to some divinely given code, or to some set of inflexible rules. The point of morality is seen as the happiness of beings in *this* world, and nothing more; and we are permitted—even required—to do whatever is necessary to promote that happiness. *That*, in its time, was a revolutionary idea.

The utilitarians were, as I said, social reformers as well as philosophers. They intended their doctrine to make a difference, not only in thought but in practice. To illustrate this, we will briefly examine the implications of their philosophy for two rather different practical issues: euthanasia and the treatment of nonhuman animals. These matters do not by any means exhaust the practical applications of Utilitarianism; nor are they necessarily the issues that utilitarians would find most pressing. But they do give a good indication of the kind of distinctive approach that Utilitarianism provides.

7.2. First Example: Euthanasia

Matthew Donnelly was a physicist who had worked with X-rays for thirty years. Perhaps as a result of too much exposure, he contracted cancer and lost part of his jaw, his upper lip, his nose, and his left hand, as well as two fingers from his right hand. He was also left blind. Mr. Donnelly's physicians told him that he had about a year left to live, but he decided that he did not want to go on living in such a state. He was in constant pain—one writer said that "at its worst, he could be seen lying in bed with teeth clinched and beads of perspiration standing out on his forehead." Knowing that he was going to die eventually anyway, and wanting to escape this misery, Mr. Donnelly begged his three brothers to kill him. Two refused, but one did not. The youngest brother, 36 year old Harold Donnelly, carried a .30-caliber pistol into the hospital and shot Matthew to death.

This, unfortunately, is a true story, and the question naturally arises whether Harold Donnelly's act was immoral. On the one hand, we may assume that Harold was motivated by noble sentiments; he loved his brother and wanted only to relieve his misery. Moreover, Matthew had *asked* to die. All this argues for a lenient judgment. Nevertheless, according to the dominant moral tradition in our society, what Harold Donnelly did was wrong.

The dominant moral tradition in our society is, of course, the Christian tradition. Christianity holds that human life is a gift from God, so that only he may decide when it will end. The early church prohibited all killing, believing that Jesus' teachings on this subject permitted no exceptions to the rule. Later, some exceptions were made, chiefly to allow capital punishment and killing in war. But other kinds of killing, including suicide and euthanasia, remained absolutely forbidden. To summarize the church's doctrine, theologians formulated a rule saying that *the intentional killing of innocent people is always wrong*. This conception has, more than any other single idea, shaped Western attitudes about the morality of killing. That is why we are so reluctant to excuse Harold Donnelly, even though he may have acted from noble motives. He intentionally killed an innocent person; therefore, according to our moral tradition, what he did was wrong.

Utilitarianism takes a very different approach. It would have us ask: Considering the choices available to Harold Donnelly, what course of conduct will have the best overall consequences? What action will produce the greatest balance of happiness over unhappiness for all concerned? The person who will be most affected will, of course, be Matthew Donnelly himself. If Harold does not kill him, he will live on, for perhaps a year, blind, mutilated, and in continuing pain. How much unhappiness would this involve? It is hard to say precisely; but Matthew Donnelly's own testimony was that he was so unhappy in this condition that he preferred death. Killing him would provide an escape from this misery. Therefore, utilitarians have concluded that euthanasia may, in such a case, be morally right. Their argument can be summarized like this:

(1) The morally right thing to do, on any occasion, is whatever would bring about the greatest balance of happiness over unhappiness.

(2) On at least some occasions, the greatest balance of happiness over unhappiness may be brought about by mercy killing.

(3) Therefore, on at least some occasions, mercy killing may be morally right.

Although this kind of argument is very different from what one finds in the Christian tradition—as I said before, it depends on no theological conceptions, and it has no use for inflexible "rules"—the classical utilitarians did not think they were advocating an atheistic or antireligious philosophy. Bentham suggests that religion would endorse, not condemn, the utilitarian viewpoint if only its adherents would take seriously their view of God as a *benevolent* creator. He writes:

> The dictates of religion would coincide, in all cases, with
> those of utility, were the Being, who is the object of reli-
> gion, universally supposed to be as benevolent as he is
> supposed to be wise and powerful. . . . But among the
> votaries of religion (of which number the multifarious
> fraternity of Christians is but a small part) there seem to
> be but few (I will not say how few) who are real believers
> in his benevolence. They call him benevolent in words,
> but they do not mean that he is so in reality.

The morality of mercy killing might be a case in point. How,
Bentham might ask, could a *benevolent* God forbid the killing
of Matthew Donnelly? If someone were to say that God is kind
but that he requires Mr. Donnelly to suffer for the additional
year before finally dying, this would be exactly what Bentham
means by "calling him benevolent in words, but not meaning
that he is so in reality."

But the majority of religious people do not agree with
Bentham; and not only our moral tradition but our legal tradition as well has evolved under the influence of Christianity.
Euthanasia is illegal, and Harold Donnelly was duly arrested
and charged with homicide. What would Utilitarianism say
about this? If, on the utilitarian view, euthanasia is moral,
should it also be made legal?

This question is connected with the more general question of what the purpose of the law ought to be. Bentham was
trained in the law, and he thought of the Principle of Utility as
a guide for legislators as well as for ordinary people making
individual moral decisions. The purpose of the law is the same
as that of morals: it should promote the general welfare of all
citizens. Bentham thought it obvious that if the law is to serve
this purpose, it should not restrict the freedom of citizens any
more than necessary. In particular, no type of activity should
be prohibited unless, in engaging in that activity, *one is doing
harm to others*. Bentham objected to laws regulating the sexual
conduct of "consenting adults," for example, on the grounds
that such conduct is not harmful to others, and because such
laws diminish rather than increase happiness. But it was Mill
who gave this principle its most eloquent expression, when he
wrote in his essay *On Liberty* (1859):

> The sole end for which mankind are warranted, individu-
> ally or collectively, in interfering with the liberty of action
> of any of their number, is self-protection. The only pur-
> pose for which power can be rightfully exercised over any
> member of a civilized community, against his will, is to
> prevent harm to others. His own good, physical or moral,
> is not a sufficient warrant. . . . Over himself, over his
> own body and mind, the individual is sovereign.

Thus for the classical utilitarians, laws prohibiting euthanasia
are not only contrary to the general welfare; they are also un-
justifiable restrictions on people's right to control their own
lives. When Harold Donnelly killed his brother, he was assisting his brother in concluding his *own* life in a manner that *he*
had chosen. No harm was caused to any other member of society, and so it was none of their business. It is worth noting
that, consistent with his philosophy, Bentham himself is said
to have requested euthanasia in his final days, although we do
not know whether this request was granted.

7.3. Second Example: Nonhuman Animals

The treatment of nonhumans has not traditionally been regarded as presenting much of a moral issue. The Christian
tradition says that man alone is made in God's image and that
mere animals do not even have souls. Thus the natural order
of things permits humans to use animals for any purpose they
see fit. St. Thomas Aquinas summed up the traditional view
when he wrote:

> Hereby is refuted the error of those who said it is sinful
> for a man to kill dumb animals: for by divine providence
> they are intended for man's use in the natural order.
> Hence it is no wrong for man to make use of them, ei-
> ther by killing them or in any other way whatever.

But isn't it wrong to be *cruel* to animals? Aquinas concedes
that it is, but he says the reason has to do with *human* welfare,
not the welfare of the animals themselves:

> If any passages of Holy Writ seem to forbid us to be cruel
> to dumb animals, for instance to kill a bird with its
> young: this is either to remove man's thoughts from

being cruel to other men, and lest through being cruel to animals one becomes cruel to human beings: or because injury to an animal leads to the temporal hurt of man, either the doer of the deed, or of another.

Thus people and animals are in entirely separate moral categories. Strictly speaking, animals have no moral standing of their own. We are free to treat them in any way that might seem to our advantage.

When it is spelled out as baldly as this, the traditional doctrine may make one a little nervous: it seems rather extreme in its lack of concern for the animals, many of whom are, after all, intelligent and sensitive creatures. Yet only a little reflection is needed to see how much our conduct is actually guided by this doctrine. We eat animals; we use them as experimental subjects in our laboratories; we use their skins for clothing and their heads as wall ornaments; we make them the objects of our amusement in zoos and rodeos; and, indeed, there is a popular sport that consists in tracking them down and killing them just for the fun of it.

If one is uncomfortable with the theological "justification" for these practices, Western philosophers have offered an abundance of secular ones. It is said, variously, that animals are not *rational*, that they lack the ability to *speak*, or that they simply are not *human*—and all these are given as reasons why their interests are outside the sphere of moral concern.

The utilitarians, however, would have none of this. On their view, what matters is not whether an individual has a soul, is rational, or any of the rest. All that matters is whether he is capable of experiencing happiness and unhappiness—pleasure and pain. If an individual *is* capable of suffering, then we have a duty to take that into account when we are deciding what to do, even if the individual in question is nonhuman. In fact, Bentham argues, whether the individual is human or nonhuman is just as irrelevant as whether he is black or white. Bentham writes:

> The day *may* come when the rest of the animal creation may acquire those rights which never could have been witholden from them but by the hand of tyranny. The French have already discovered that the blackness of the

skin is no reason why a human being should be abandoned without redress to the caprice of a tormentor. It
may one day come to be recognized that the number of
the legs, the villosity of the skin, or the termination of
the *os sacrum* are reasons equally insufficient for abandoning a sensitive being to the same fate. What else is it
that should trace the insuperable line? Is it the faculty of
reason, or perhaps the faculty of discourse? But a full-
grown horse or dog is beyond comparison a more rational, as well as a more conversable animal, than an infant
of a day or a week or even a month, old. But suppose
they were otherwise, what would it avail? The question is
not, Can they *reason?* nor Can they *talk?* but, *Can they suffer?*

Mill, in the passage quoted on page 92, makes the same point
in a more general way. He describes morality as the "rules and
precepts for human conduct" by which a pleasurable existence "might be . . . secured to all mankind, *and not to them
only, but, so far as the nature of things admits, to the whole of sentient creation.*"

Because humans and nonhumans can suffer, we have the
same reason for not mistreating both. If a human is tormented, why is it wrong? Because he suffers. Similarly, if a
nonhuman is tormented, he also suffers, and so it is equally
wrong for the same reason. To Bentham and Mill, this line of
reasoning was conclusive. Humans and nonhumans are in exactly the same moral category.

However, this view may seem as extreme, in the opposite
direction, as the traditional view that gives animals no independent moral standing at all. Are animals really to be regarded as the *equals* of humans? In some ways Bentham and
Mill thought so, but they were careful to point out that this
does not mean that animals and humans must always be
treated in the same way. There are factual differences between
them that often will justify differences in treatment. For example, because humans have intellectual capacities that animals
lack, they are able to take pleasure in things that nonhumans
cannot enjoy—humans can do mathematics, appreciate literature, and so on. And similarly, their superior capacities might
make them capable of frustrations and disappointments that

other animals are not able to experience. Thus our duty to promote happiness entails a duty to promote those special enjoyments for them, as well as to prevent any special unhappinesses to which they are vulnerable. At the same time, however, insofar as the welfare of other animals *is* affected by our conduct, we have a strict moral duty to take that into account, and their suffering counts equally with any similar suffering experienced by a human.

Contemporary utilitarians have sometimes resisted this aspect of the classical doctrine, and that is not surprising. Our "right" to kill, experiment on, and otherwise use animals as we please seems to most of us so obvious that it is hard to believe we really are behaving as immorally as Bentham and Mill suggest. Some contemporary utilitarians, however, have produced powerful arguments that Bentham and Mill were right. The Australian philosopher Peter Singer, in a book with the odd-sounding title *Animal Liberation* (1975), has urged, following the principles laid down by Bentham and Mill, that our treatment of nonhuman animals is deeply objectionable.

Singer asks how we can possibly justify experiments such as this one:

> At Harvard University R. Solomon, L. Kamin, and L. Wynne tested the effects of electric shock on the behavior of dogs. They placed forty dogs in a device called a "shuttlebox" which consists of a box divided into two compartments, separated by a barrier. Initially the barrier was set at the height of the dog's back. Hundreds of intense electric shocks were delivered to the dogs' feet through a grid floor. At first the dogs could escape the shock if they learned to jump the barrier into the other compartment. In an attempt to "discourage" one dog from jumping, the experimenters forced the dog to jump *into* shock 100 times. They said that as the dog jumped he gave a "sharp anticipatory yip which turned into a yelp when he landed on the electrified grid." They then blocked the passage between the compartments with a piece of plate glass and tested the same dog again. The dog "jumped forward and smashed his head against the glass." Initially dogs showed symptoms such as "defecation, urination, yelping and shrieking, trembling, attacking the apparatus" and so on, but after ten or twelve days

of trials dogs that were prevented from escaping shock ceased to resist. The experimenters reported themselves "impressed" by this, and concluded that a combination of the plate glass barrier and foot shock were "very effective" in eliminating jumping by dogs.

The utilitarian argument is simple enough. We should judge actions right or wrong depending on whether they cause more happiness or unhappiness. The dogs in this experiment are obviously being caused terrible suffering. Is there any compensating gain in happiness elsewhere that justifies it? Is *greater* unhappiness being prevented, for other animals or for humans? If not, the experiment is not morally acceptable. We may note that this style of argument does not imply that all such experiments are immoral—it suggests judging each one individually, on its own merits. But it *does* insist that the pain caused to the animals requires justification. We cannot simply assume, because they are not human, that anything goes.

But criticizing such experiments is too easy for most of us. Because *we* are not involved in the experiments, we may feel superior or self-righteous. Singer points out, however, that none of us is free of blame in this area. We are all involved in cruelty just as serious as that perpetrated in any laboratory, because we all (or, at least most of us) participate in the business of meat eating. The facts about meat production are at least as harrowing as the facts about animal experimentation.

Most people believe, in a vague way, that while the slaughterhouse may be an unpleasant place, the animals that are raised for food are otherwise treated well enough. But, Singer's argument points out, nothing could be further from the truth. Veal calves, for example, spend their lives in pens too small to allow them to turn around or even to lie down comfortably—but from the producers' point of view, that is good, because exercise toughens the muscles, which reduces the "quality" of the meat; and besides, allowing the animals adequate living space would be prohibitively expensive. In these pens the calves cannot perform such basic actions as grooming themselves, which they naturally desire to do, because there is not room for them to twist their heads around. It is clear that the calves miss their mothers, and like human infants they want something to suck: they can be seen trying vainly to suck the sides of their stalls. In order to keep their meat pale and tasty, they are fed a liquid diet deficient in both iron and roughage. Naturally they develop cravings for these things. The calf's craving for iron becomes so strong that if allowed to turn around, it will lick at its own urine, although calves normally find this repugnant. The tiny stall, which prevents the animal from turning, solves this "problem." The craving for roughage is especially strong, since without it the animal cannot form a cud to chew. It cannot be given any straw for bedding, since the animal would be driven to eat it, and that would affect the meat. So for these animals, the slaughterhouse is not an unpleasant end to an otherwise contented existence. As terrifying as the process of slaughter is, for them it may actually be a merciful release.

Once again, given these facts, the utilitarian argument is simple enough. The system of meat production causes great suffering for the animals. Because we do not *need* to eat them—vegetarian meals are also tasty and nourishing—the good that is done does not, on balance, outweigh the evil. Therefore, it is wrong. Singer concludes that we should become vegetarians.

What is most revolutionary in all this is simply the idea that the interests of nonhuman animals *count*. We normally assume, as the dominant tradition of our society teaches, that human beings alone are worthy of moral consideration. Utilitarianism challenges that basic assumption and insists that the moral community must be expanded to include all creatures whose interests are affected by what we do. Human beings are in many ways special; and an adequate morality must acknowledge that. But it is also true that we are only one species among many inhabiting this planet; and morality must acknowledge *that* as well.

CHAPTER 8

The Debate over Utilitarianism

The utilitarian doctrine is that happiness is desirable, and the only thing desirable, as an end; all other things being desirable as means to that end.

JOHN STUART MILL, *UTILITARIANISM* (1861)

Man does not strive after happiness; only the Englishman does that.

FRIEDRICH NIETZSCHE, *TWILIGHT OF THE IDOLS* (1889)

8.1. The Resilience of the Theory

Classical Utilitarianism—the theory defended by Bentham and Mill—can be summarized in three propositions:

First, actions are to be judged right or wrong solely in virtue of their consequences. Nothing else matters. Right actions are, simply, those that have the best consequences.

Second, in assessing consequences, the only thing that matters is the amount of happiness or unhappiness that is caused. Everything else is irrelevant. Thus right actions are those that produce the greatest balance of happiness over unhappiness.

Third, in calculating the happiness or unhappiness that will be caused, no one's happiness is to be counted as more important than anyone else's. Each person's welfare is equally important. As Mill put it in his *Utilitarianism,*

> the happiness which forms the utilitarian standard of what is right in conduct, is not the agent's own happiness, but that of all concerned. As between his own happiness and that of others, utilitarianism requires him to

be as strictly impartial as a disinterested and benevolent spectator.

Thus right actions are those that produce the greatest possible balance of happiness over unhappiness, with each person's happiness counted as equally important.

The appeal of this theory to philosophers, economists, and others who theorize about human decision making has been enormous. The theory continues to be widely accepted, even though it has been challenged by a number of apparently devastating arguments. These antiutilitarian arguments are so numerous, and so persuasive, that many have concluded the theory must be abandoned. But the remarkable thing is that so many have *not* abandoned it. Despite the arguments, a great many thinkers refuse to let the theory go. According to these contemporary utilitarians, the antiutilitarian arguments show only that the classical theory needs to be *modified;* they say the basic idea is correct and should be preserved, but recast into a more satisfactory form.

In what follows, we will examine some of these arguments against Utilitarianism, and consider whether the classical version of the theory may be revised satisfactorily to meet them. These arguments are of interest not only for the assessment of Utilitarianism but for their own sakes, as they raise some additional fundamental issues of moral philosophy.

8.2. Is Happiness the Only Thing That Matters?

The question *What things are good?* is different from the question *What actions are right?* and Utilitarianism answers the second question by referring back to the first one. Right actions, it says, are the ones that produce the most good. But what is good? The classical utilitarian reply is: one thing, and one thing only, namely happiness. As Mill put it, "The utilitarian doctrine is that happiness is desirable, and the only thing desirable, as an end; all other things being desirable as means to that end."

The idea that happiness is the one ultimate good (and

unhappiness the one ultimate evil) is known as *Hedonism*. Hedonism is a perennially popular theory that goes back at least as far as the ancient Greeks. It has always been an attractive theory because of its beautiful simplicity, and because it expresses the intuitively plausible notion that things are good or bad only on account of the way they make us *feel*. Yet a little reflection reveals serious flaws in the theory. The flaws stand out when we consider examples like these:

1. A promising young pianist's hands are injured in an automobile accident so that she can no longer play. Why is this a bad thing for her? Hedonism would say it is bad because it causes her unhappiness. She will feel frustrated and upset whenever she thinks of what might have been, and *that* is her misfortune. But this way of explaining the misfortune seems to get things the wrong way around. It is not as though, by feeling unhappy, she has made an otherwise neutral situation into a bad one. On the contrary, her unhappiness is a rational response to a situation that *is* unfortunate. She could have had a career as a concert pianist, and now she cannot. *That* is the tragedy. We could not eliminate the tragedy just by getting her to cheer up.

2. You think someone is your friend, but really he ridicules you behind your back. No one ever tells you, so you never know. Is this situation unfortunate for you? Hedonism would have to say no, because you are never caused any unhappiness by the situation. Yet we do feel that there is something bad going on here. You *think* he is your friend, and you are "being made a fool," even though you are not aware of it and so suffer no unhappiness.

Both these examples make the same basic point. We value all sorts of things, including artistic creativity and friendship, for their own sakes. It makes us happy to have them, but only because we *already* think them good. (We do not think them good *because* they make us happy—this is what I meant when I said that Hedonism "gets things the wrong way around.") Therefore we think it a misfortune to lose them, independently of whether or not the loss is accompanied by unhappiness.

In this way, Hedonism misunderstands the nature of happiness. Happiness is not something that is recognized as good and sought for its own sake, with other things appreciated only as means of bringing it about. Instead, happiness is a response we have to the attainment of things that we recognize *as* goods, independently and in their own right. We think that friendship is a good thing, and so having friends makes us happy. That is very different from first setting out after happiness, then deciding that having friends might make us happy, and then seeking friends as a means to this end.

Today, most philosophers recognize the truth of this. There are not many contemporary hedonists. Those sympathetic to Utilitarianism have therefore sought a way to formulate their view without assuming a hedonistic account of good and evil. Some, such as the English philosopher G. E. Moore (1873–1958), have tried to compile short lists of things to be regarded as good in themselves. Moore suggested that there are three obvious intrinsic goods—pleasure, friendship, and aesthetic enjoyment—and that right actions are those that increase the world's supply of such things. Other utilitarians have tried to bypass the question of how many things are good in themselves, leaving it an open question and saying only that right actions are the ones that have the best results, *however* goodness is measured. Still others try to bypass the question in another way, holding only that we should act so as to maximize the satisfaction of people's *preferences*. It is beyond the scope of this book to discuss the merits or demerits of these varieties of Utilitarianism. I mention them only in order to note that although the hedonistic assumption of the classical utilitarians has largely been rejected, contemporary utilitarians have not found it difficult to carry on. They do so by urging that Hedonism was never a necessary part of the theory in the first place.

8.3. Are Consequences All That Matter?

The claim that only consequences matter *is*, however, a necessary part of Utilitarianism. The most fundamental idea underlying the theory is that in order to determine whether an action would be right, we should look at *what will happen as a result of doing it*. If it were to turn out that some *other* matter is also important in determining rightness, then Utilitarianism would be undermined at its very foundation.

The most serious antiutilitarian arguments attack the theory at just this point: they urge that various other considerations, in addition to utility, are important in determining whether actions are right. We will look briefly at three such arguments.

1. *Justice.* Writing in the academic journal *Inquiry* in 1965, H. J. McCloskey asks us to consider the following case:

> Suppose a utilitarian were visiting an area in which there was racial strife, and that, during his visit, a Negro rapes a white woman, and that race riots occur as a result of the crime, white mobs, with the connivance of the police, bashing and killing Negroes, etc. Suppose too that our utilitarian is in the area of the crime when it is committed such that his testimony would bring about the conviction of a particular Negro. If he knows that a quick arrest will stop the riots and lynchings, surely, as a utilitarian, he must conclude that he has a duty to bear false witness in order to bring about the punishment of an innocent person.

This is a fictitious example, but that makes no difference. The argument is only that *if* someone were in this position, then on utilitarian grounds he should bear false witness against the innocent person. This might have some bad consequences— the innocent man might be executed—but there would be enough good consequences to outweigh them: the riots and lynchings would be stopped. The best consequences would be achieved by lying; therefore, according to Utilitarianism, lying is the thing to do. But, the argument continues, it would be wrong to bring about the execution of the innocent man. Therefore, Utilitarianism, which implies it would be right, must be incorrect.

According to the critics of Utilitarianism, this argument illustrates one of the theory's most serious shortcomings: namely, that it is incompatible with the ideal of justice. Justice requires that we treat people fairly, according to their individual needs and merits. The innocent man has done nothing wrong; he did not commit the rape and so he does not deserve to be punished for it. Therefore, punishing him would be unjust. The example illustrates how the demands of justice and the demands of utility can come into conflict, and so a theory that says utility is the *whole* story cannot be right.

2. *Rights.* Here is a case that is *not* fictitious; it is from the records of the U.S. Court of Appeals, Ninth Circuit (Southern District of California), 1963, in the case of *York* v. *Story:*

> In October, 1958, appellant [Ms. Angelynn York] went to the police department of Chino for the purpose of filing charges in connection with an assault upon her. Appellee Ron Story, an officer of that police department, then acting under color of his authority as such, advised appellant that it was necessary to take photographs of her. Story then took appellant to a room in the police station, locked the door, and directed her to undress, which she did. Story then directed appellant to assume various indecent positions, and photographed her in those positions. These photographs were not made for any lawful purpose.
>
> Appellant objected to undressing. She stated to Story that there was no need to take photographs of her in the nude, or in the positions she was directed to take, because the bruises would not show in any photograph. . . .
>
> Later that month, Story advised appellant that the pictures did not come out and that he had destroyed them. Instead, Story circulated these photographs among the personnel of the Chino police department. In April, 1960, two other officers of that police department, appellee Louis Moreno and defendant Henry Grote, acting under color of their authority as such, and using police photographic equipment located at the police station made additional prints of the photographs taken by Story. Moreno and Grote then circulated these prints among the personnel of the Chino police department. . . .

Ms. York brought suit against these officers and won. Her *legal* rights had clearly been violated. But what of the *morality* of the officers' behavior?

Utilitarianism says that actions are defensible if they produce a favorable balance of happiness over unhappiness. This suggests that we consider the amount of unhappiness caused to Ms. York and compare it with the amount of pleasure taken in the photographs by Officer Story and his cohorts. It is at least possible that more happiness than unhappiness was caused. In that case, the utilitarian conclusion apparently would be that their actions were morally all right. But this seems to be a perverse way to approach the case. Why should the pleasure afforded Story and his cohorts matter at all? Why should it even count? They had no right to treat Ms. York in that way, and the fact that they enjoyed doing so hardly seems a relevant defense.

To make the point even clearer, consider an (imaginary) related case. Suppose a Peeping Tom spied on Ms. York by peering through her bedroom window, and secretly took pictures of her undressed. Further suppose that he did this without ever being detected and that he used the photographs entirely for his own amusement, without showing them to anyone. Now under these circumstances, it seems clear that the *only* consequence of his action is an increase in his own happiness. No one else, including Ms. York, is caused any unhappiness at all. How, then, could Utilitarianism deny that the Peeping Tom's actions are right? But it is evident to moral common sense that they are not right. Thus, Utilitarianism appears to be an incorrect moral view.

The moral to be drawn from this argument is that Utilitarianism is at odds with the idea that people have *rights* that may not be trampled on merely because one anticipates good results. This is an extremely important notion, which explains why a great many philosophers have rejected Utilitarianism. In the above cases, it is Ms. York's right to privacy that is violated; but it would not be difficult to think of similar cases in which other rights are at issue—the right to freedom of religion, to free speech, or even the right to life itself. It may happen that good purposes are served, from time to time, by ignoring these rights. But we do not think that our rights *should* be set aside so easily. The notion of a personal right is not a utilitarian notion. Quite the reverse: it is a notion that places limits on how an individual may be treated, regardless of the good purposes that might be accomplished.

3. *Backward-Looking Reasons.* Suppose you have promised someone you will do something—say, you promised to meet

him downtown this afternoon. But when the time comes to go, you don't want to do it—you need to do some work and would rather stay home. What should you do? Suppose you judge that the utility of getting your work accomplished slightly outweighs the inconvenience your friend would be caused. Appealing to the utilitarian standard, you might then conclude that it is right to stay home. However, this does not seem correct. The fact that *you promised* imposes an obligation on you that you cannot escape so easily. Of course, if the consequences of not breaking the promise were *great*—if, for example, your mother had just been stricken with a heart attack and you had to rush her to the hospital—you would be justified in breaking it. But a *small* gain in utility cannot overcome the obligation imposed by the fact that you promised. Thus Utilitarianism, which says that consequences are the only things that matter, seems mistaken.

There is an important general lesson to be learned from this argument. Why is Utilitarianism vulnerable to this sort of criticism? It is because the only kinds of considerations that the theory holds relevant to determining the rightness of actions are considerations having to do with the *future*. Because of its exclusive concern with consequences, Utilitarianism has us confine our attention to what *will happen* as a result of our actions. However, we normally think that considerations about the *past* also have some importance. The fact that you promised your friend to meet him is a fact about the past, not the future. Therefore, the general point to be made about Utilitarianism is that it seems to be an inadequate moral theory because it excludes what we might call backward-looking considerations.

Once we understand this point, other examples of backward-looking considerations come easily to mind. The fact that someone did not commit a crime is a good reason why he should not be punished. The fact that someone once did you a favor may be a good reason why you should now do him a favor. The fact that you did something to hurt someone may be a reason why you should now make it up to her. These are all facts about the past that are relevant to determining our obligations. But Utilitarianism makes the past irrelevant, and so it seems deficient for just that reason.

8.4. The Defense of Utilitarianism

Taken together, the above arguments form an impressive in-
dictment of Utilitarianism. The theory, which at first seemed
so progressive and commonsensical, now seems indefensible:
it is at odds with such fundamental moral notions as justice
and individual rights, and seems unable to account for the
place of backward-looking reasons in justifying conduct. The
combined weight of these arguments has prompted many
philosophers to abandon the theory altogether.

Many thinkers, however, continue to believe that Utilitarianism, in some form, is true. In reply to the arguments, three
general defenses have been offered.

The First Line of Defense. The first line of defense is to point
out that the examples used in the antiutilitarian arguments
are unrealistic and do not describe situations that come up in
the real world. Since Utilitarianism is designed as a guide for
decision making in the situations we actually face, the fanciful
examples are dismissed as irrelevant.

The three antiutilitarian arguments share a common
strategy. First a case is described, and then it is noted that
from a utilitarian point of view a certain action seems to be required—that is, a certain action would have the best consequences. It is then said that this action is not right. Therefore,
it is concluded, the utilitarian conception of rightness cannot
be correct.

This strategy succeeds only if we admit that the actions
described *really would* have the best consequences. But the
utilitarian need not admit this. He can object that, in the real
world, bearing false witness does *not* have good consequences.
Suppose, in the case described by McCloskey, the "utilitarian"
tried to incriminate the innocent man in order to stop the
riots. His effort might not succeed; his lie might be found out,
and then the situation would be even worse than before. Even
if the lie did succeed, the real culprit would remain at large,
to commit additional crimes. Moreover, if the guilty party
were caught later on, which is always a possibility, the liar
would be in deep trouble, and confidence in the criminal justice system would be undermined. The moral is that although

one might *think* that one can bring about the best consequences by such behavior, one can by no means be certain of
it. In fact, experience teaches the contrary: utility is not
served by framing innocent people. Thus the utilitarian position is *not* at odds with common-sense notions of justice in
such cases.

The same goes for the other cases cited in the antiutilitarian arguments. Violating people's rights, breaking one's
promises, and lying all have bad consequences. Only in
philosophers' imaginations is it otherwise. In the real world,
Peeping Toms are caught, just as Officer Story and his cohorts
were caught; and their victims suffer. In the real world, when
people lie, others are hurt and their own reputations are damaged; and when people break their promises, they lose their
friends.

Therefore, far from being incompatible with the idea
that we should not violate people's rights or lie or break our
promises, Utilitarianism explains *why* we should not do those
things. Moreover, apart from the utilitarian explanation, these
duties would remain mysterious and unintelligible. What
could be more mysterious than the notion that some actions
are right "in themselves," severed from any notion of a good
to be produced by them? Or what could be more unintelligible than the idea that people have "rights" unconnected with
any benefits derived from the acknowledgment of those
rights? Utilitarianism is not incompatible with common sense;
on the contrary, Utilitarianism *is* commonsensical.

The Second Line of Defense. The first line of defense contains more bluster than substance. While it can plausibly be
maintained that *most* acts of false witness and the like have
bad consequences in the real world, it cannot reasonably be
asserted that *all* such acts have bad consequences. Surely, in at
least some real-life cases, one can bring about good results by
doing things that moral common sense condemns. Therefore,
in at least some real-life cases Utilitarianism will come into
conflict with common sense. Moreover, even if the antiutilitarian arguments had to rely exclusively on fictitious examples,
those arguments would nevertheless retain their power; for
showing that Utilitarianism has unacceptable consequences in

hypothetical cases is a perfectly valid way of pointing up its theoretical defects. The first line of defense, then, is weak.

The second line of defense admits all this and proposes to save Utilitarianism by giving it a new formulation. In revising a theory to meet criticism, the trick is to identify precisely the feature of the theory that is causing the trouble and to change *that,* leaving the rest of the theory undisturbed as much as possible.

The troublesome aspect of the theory was this: the classical version of Utilitarianism implied that *each individual action* is to be evaluated by reference to its own particular consequences. If on a certain occasion you are tempted to lie, whether it would be wrong is determined by the consequences of *that particular lie.* This, the theory's defenders said, is the point that causes all the trouble; even though we know that *in general* lying has bad consequences, it is obvious that sometimes particular acts of lying can have good consequences.

Therefore, the new version of Utilitarianism modifies the theory so that individual actions will no longer be judged by the Principle of Utility. Instead, *rules* will be established by reference to the principle, and individual acts will then be judged right or wrong by reference to the rules. This new version of the theory is called *Rule-Utilitarianism,* to contrast it with the original theory, now commonly called *Act-Utilitarianism.*

Rule-Utilitarianism has no difficulty coping with the three anti-utilitarian arguments. An act-utilitarian, faced with the situation described by McCloskey, would be tempted to bear false witness against the innocent man because the consequences of *that particular act* would be good. But the rule-utilitarian would not reason in that way. He would first ask, "What *general rules of conduct* tend to promote the greatest happiness?" Suppose we imagine two societies, one in which the rule "Don't bear false witness against the innocent" is faithfully adhered to, and one in which this rule is not followed. In which society are people likely to be better off? Clearly, from the point of view of utility, the first society is preferable. Therefore, the rule against incriminating the innocent should be accepted, and *by appealing to this rule,* the rule-utilitarian concludes that the person in McCloskey's example should not testify against the innocent man.

Analogous arguments can be used to establish rules against violating people's rights, breaking promises, lying, and so on. We should accept such rules because following them, as a regular practice, promotes the general welfare. But once having appealed to the Principle of Utility to establish the rules, we do not have to invoke the principle again to determine the rightness of particular actions. Individual actions are justified simply by appeal to the already-established rules.

Thus Rule-Utilitarianism cannot be convicted of violating our moral common sense, or of conflicting with ordinary ideas of justice, personal rights, and the rest. In shifting emphasis from the justification of acts to the justification of rules, the theory has been brought into line with our intuitive judgments to a remarkable degree.

The Third Line of Defense. Finally, a small group of contemporary utilitarians has had a very different response to the anti-utilitarian arguments. Those arguments point out that the classical theory is at odds with ordinary notions of justice, individual rights, and so on; to this, their response is, essentially, "So what?" In 1961 the Australian philosopher J. J. C. Smart published a monograph entitled *An Outline of a System of Utilitarian Ethics;* reflecting on his position in that book, Smart said:

> Admittedly utilitarianism does have consequences which are incompatible with the common moral consciousness, but I tended to take the view "so much the worse for the common moral consciousness." That is, I was inclined to reject the common methodology of testing general ethical principles by seeing how they square with our feelings in particular instances.

Our moral common sense is, after all, not necessarily reliable. It may incorporate various irrational elements, including prejudices absorbed from our parents, our religion, and the general culture. Why should we simply assume that our feelings are always correct? And why should we reject a plausible, rational theory of ethics such as Utilitarianism simply because it conflicts with those feelings? Perhaps it is the feelings, not the theory, that should be discarded.

In light of this, consider again McCloskey's example of the person tempted to bear false witness. McCloskey argues that it would be wrong to have a man convicted of a crime he did not commit, because it would be unjust. But wait: such a judgment serves *that man's* interests well enough, but what of the *other* innocent people who will be hurt if the rioting and lynchings are allowed to continue? What of them? Surely we might hope that we never have to face a situation like this, for the options are all extremely distasteful. But if we *must* choose between (a) securing the conviction of one innocent person and (b) allowing the deaths of several innocent people, is it so unreasonable to think that the first option, bad as it is, is preferable to the second?

On this way of thinking, Act-Utilitarianism is a perfectly defensible doctrine and does not need to be modified. Rule-Utilitarianism, by contrast, is an unnecessarily watered-down version of the theory, which gives rules a greater importance than they merit. Act-Utilitarianism is, however, recognized to be a radical doctrine which implies that many of our ordinary moral feelings may be mistaken. In this respect, it does what good philosophy always does—it challenges us to rethink matters that we have heretofore taken for granted.

8.5. What Is Correct and What Is Incorrect in Utilitarianism

There is a sense in which no moral philosopher can completely reject Utilitarianism. The consequences of one's actions—whether they promote happiness, or cause misery—must be admitted by all to be extremely important. John Stuart Mill once remarked that, insofar as we are benevolent, we must accept the utilitarian standard; and he was surely right. Moreover, the utilitarian emphasis on impartiality must also be a part of any defensible moral theory. The question is whether these are the *only* kinds of considerations an adequate theory must acknowledge. Aren't there *other* considerations that are also important?

If we consult what Smart calls our "common moral consciousness," it seems that there are *many* other considerations that are morally important. (In section 8.3 above, we looked at a few examples.) But I believe the radical act-utilitarians are right to warn us that "common sense" cannot be trusted. Many people once felt that there is an important difference between whites and blacks, so that the interests of whites are somehow more important. Trusting the "common sense" of their day, they might have insisted that an adequate moral theory should accommodate this "fact." Today, no one worth listening to would say such a thing. But who knows how many *other* irrational prejudices are still a part of our moral common sense? At the end of his classic study of race relations, *An American Dilemma* (1944), the Swedish sociologist Gunnar Myrdal reminds us:

> There must be still other countless errors of the same sort that no living man can yet detect, because of the fog within which our type of Western culture envelops us. Cultural influences have set up the assumptions about the mind, the body, and the universe with which we begin; pose the questions we ask; influence the facts we seek; determine the interpretation we give these facts; and direct our reaction to these interpretations and conclusions.

The strength of Utilitarianism is that it firmly resists "corruption" by possibly irrational elements. By sticking to the Principle of Utility as the *only* standard for judging right and wrong, it avoids all danger of incorporating into moral theory prejudices, feelings, and "intuitions" that have no rational basis.

The warning should be heeded. "Common sense" can, indeed, mislead us. At the same time, however, there might be at least some nonutilitarian considerations that an adequate theory *should* accept, because there *is* a rational basis for them. Consider, for example, the matter of what people deserve. A person who has worked hard in her job may deserve a promotion more than someone who has loafed, and it would be unjust for the loafer to be promoted first. This is a point that we would expect any fair-minded employer to acknowledge; we would all be indignant if we were passed over for promotion in favor of someone who had not worked as hard or as well as we. Now utilitarians might agree with this, and say that it can be explained by their theory—they might argue that it promotes the general welfare to encourage hard work by rewarding it. But this does not seem to be an adequate explanation of the importance of desert. The woman who worked harder has a superior claim to the promotion, *not* because it promotes the general welfare for her to get it, but *because she has earned it.* The reason she should be promoted has to do with *her* merits. This does not appear to be the kind of consideration a utilitarian could admit.

Does this way of thinking express a mere prejudice, or does it have a rational basis? I believe it has a rational basis, although it is not one that utilitarians could accept. We ought to recognize individual desert as a reason for treating people in certain ways—for example, as a reason for promoting the woman who has worked harder—because that is the principal way we have of treating individuals as autonomous, responsible beings. If in fact people have the power to choose their own actions, in such a way that they are *responsible* for those actions and what results from them, then acknowledging their deserts is just a way of acknowledging their standing as autonomous individuals. In treating them as they deserve to be treated, we are responding to the way they have freely chosen to behave. Thus in some instances we will not treat everyone alike, because people are not just members of an undifferentiated crowd. Instead, they are individuals who, by their own choices, show themselves to deserve different kinds of responses.

I will say more about what people deserve, and why this is important for ethics, in Chapters 10 and 13. Here I will draw only this conclusion about Utilitarianism: although it emphasizes points that any adequate moral theory must acknowledge, Utilitarianism is not itself a fully adequate theory because there is at least one important matter—individual desert—that escapes its net.

CHAPTER 9

Are There Absolute Moral Rules?

In spite of its horrifying title Kant's *Groundwork of the Metaphysics of Morals* is one of the small books which are truly great: it has exercised on human thought an influence almost ludicrously disproportionate to its size.

H. J. PATON, *THE MORAL LAW* (1948)

9.1. Kant and The Categorical Imperative

Imagine that someone is fleeing from a murderer and tells you he is going home to hide. Then the murderer comes along and asks where the first man went. You believe that if you tell the truth, the murderer will find his victim and kill him. What should you do—should you tell the truth or lie?

We might call this The Case of the Inquiring Murderer. In this case, most of us would think it is obvious what we should do: we should lie. Of course, we don't think we should go about lying as a general rule, but in these specific circumstances it seems the right thing to do. After all, we might say, which is more important, telling the truth or saving someone's life? Surely in a case such as *this* lying is justified.

There is one important philosopher, however, who thought we should *never* lie, even in a case such as this. Immanuel Kant (1724–1804) was one of the seminal figures in modern philosophy. Almost alone among the great thinkers, Kant believed that morality is a matter of following *absolute rules*—rules that admit no exceptions, that must be followed come what may. He believed, for example, that lying is never right, no matter what the circumstances. It is hard to see how such a radical view could be defended, unless, perhaps, one held that such rules are God's unconditional commands. But Kant did not appeal to theological considerations; he relied only on rational arguments, holding that *reason* requires that we never lie. Let us see how he reached this remarkable conclusion. First we will look briefly at his general theory of ethics.

Kant observed that the word "ought" is often used non-morally. For example:

1. If you want to become a better chess player, you ought to study the games of Bobby Fischer.
2. If you want to go to law school, you ought to sign up to take the entrance examination.

Much of our conduct is governed by such "oughts." The pattern is: we have a certain wish (to become a better chess player, to go to law school); we recognize that a certain course of action would help us get what we want (studying Fischer's games, signing up for the entrance examination); and so we conclude that we should follow the indicated plan.

Kant called these "hypothetical imperatives" because they tell us what to do *provided that* we have the relevant desires. A person who did not want to improve his or her chess would have no reason to study Fischer's games; someone who did not want to go to law school would have no reason to take the entrance examination. Because the binding force of the "ought" depends on our having the relevant desire, we can *escape* its force simply by renouncing the desire. Thus by saying "I no longer want to go to law school," one can get out of the obligation to take the exam.

Moral obligations, by contrast, do not depend on our having particular desires. The form of a moral obligation is not "If you want so-and-so, then you ought to do such-and-such." Instead, moral requirements are *categorical:* they have the form, "You ought to do such-and-such, *period.*" The moral rule is not, for example, that you ought to help people *if* you care for them or *if* you have some other purpose that helping them might serve. Instead, the rule is that you should be helpful to people *regardless of* your particular wants and desires. That is why, unlike hypothetical "oughts," moral requirements cannot be escaped simply by saying "But I don't care about that."

Hypothetical "oughts" are easy to understand. They merely require us to adopt the means that are necessary to attain the ends we choose to seek. Categorical "oughts," on the other hand, are rather mysterious. How can we be obligated to behave in a certain way regardless of the ends we wish to achieve? Much of Kant's moral philosophy is an attempt to explain what categorical "oughts" are and how they are possible.

Kant holds that, just as hypothetical "oughts" are possible because we have desires, categorical "oughts" are possible because we have reason. Categorical "oughts" are binding on rational agents *simply because they are rational.* How can this be so? It is, Kant says, because categorical oughts are derived from a principle that every rational person must accept. He calls this principle *The Categorical Imperative.* In his *Groundwork of the Metaphysics of Morals* (1785), he expresses The Categorical Imperative like this:

> Act only according to that maxim by which you can at the same time will that it should become a universal law.

This principle summarizes a procedure for deciding whether an act is morally permissible. When you are contemplating doing a particular action, you are to ask what rule you would be following if you were to do that action. (This will be the "maxim" of the act.) Then you are to ask whether you would be willing for that rule to be followed by everyone all the time. (That would make it a "universal law" in the relevant sense.) If so, the rule may be followed, and the act is permissible. However, if you would *not* be willing for everyone to follow the rule, then you may not follow it, and the act is morally impermissible.

Kant gives several examples to explain how this works. Suppose, he says, a man needs to borrow money, and he knows that no one will lend it to him unless he promises to repay. But he also knows that he will be unable to repay. He therefore faces this question: Should he promise to repay the debt, knowing that he cannot do so, in order to persuade someone to make the loan? If he were to do that, the "maxim of the act" (the rule he would be following) would be: *Whenever you need a loan, promise to repay it, even though you know you cannot do so*. Now, could this rule become a universal law? Obviously not, because it would be self-defeating. Once this became a universal practice, no one would any longer believe such promises, and so no one would make loans because of them. As Kant himself puts it, "no one would believe what was promised to him but would only laugh at any such assertion as vain pretense."

Another of Kant's examples has to do with giving charity. Suppose, he says, someone refuses to help others in need, saying to himself "What concern of mine is it? Let each one be happy as heaven wills, or as he can make himself; I will not take anything from him or even envy him; but to his welfare or to his assistance in time of need I have no desire to contribute." This, again, is a rule that one cannot will to be a universal law. For at some time in the future this man might *himself* be in need of assistance from others, and he would not want others to be so indifferent to him.

9.2. Absolute Rules and the Duty Not to Lie

Being a moral agent, then, means guiding one's conduct by "universal laws"—moral rules that hold, without exception, in all circumstances. Kant thought that the rule against lying was one such rule. Of course, this was not the *only* absolute rule Kant defended—he thought there are many others; morality is full of them. But it will be useful to focus on the rule against lying as a convenient example. Kant devoted considerable space to discussing this rule, and it is clear that he felt especially strongly about it—he said that lying in any circumstances is "the obliteration of one's dignity as a human being."

Kant offered two main arguments for this view. Let us examine them one at a time.

1. His primary reason for thinking that lying is always wrong was that the prohibition of lying follows straightaway from The Categorical Imperative. We could not will that it be a universal law that we should lie, because it would be self-defeating; people would quickly learn that they could not rely on what other people said, and so the lies would not be be-

lieved. Surely there is something to this: in order for a lie to be successful, people must believe that others are telling the truth; so the success of a lie depends on there *not* being a "universal law" permitting it.

There is, however, an important problem with this argument, which will become clear if we spell out Kant's line of thought more fully. Let us return to The Case of the Inquiring Murderer. Should you tell him the truth? Kant would have you reason as follows:

(1) You should do only those actions that conform to rules that you could will to be adopted universally.

(2) If you were to lie, you would be following the rule "It is permissible to lie."

(3) This rule could not be adopted universally, because it would be self-defeating: people would stop believing one another, and then it would do no good to lie.

(4) Therefore, you should not lie.

The problem with this way of reasoning was nicely summarized by the British philosopher Elizabeth Anscombe when she wrote about Kant in the academic journal *Philosophy* in 1958:

> His own rigoristic convictions on the subject of lying were so intense that it never occurred to him that a lie could be relevantly described as anything but just a lie (e.g., as "a lie in such-and-such circumstances"). His rule about universalizable maxims is useless without stipulations as to what shall count as a relevant description of an action with a view to constructing a maxim about it.

The difficulty arises in step (2) of the argument. Exactly what rule would you be following if you lied? The crucial point is that there are many ways to formulate the rule; some of them might not be "universalizable" in Kant's sense, but some would be. Suppose we said you were following *this* rule (R): "It is permissible to lie when doing so would save someone's life." We *could* will that (R) be made a "universal law," and it would not be self-defeating.

It might be replied that the universal adoption of (R) *would* be self-defeating because potential murderers would cease to believe us. But they would believe us if they thought we did not know what they were up to; and if they thought we *did* know what they were up to, they would not bother to ask us in the first place. This is no different from the situation that exists now, in the real world: murderers know that people will not willingly aid them. Thus the adoption of (R) would help save lives, at little cost, and it would not undermine general confidence in what people say in ordinary circumstances.

2. The Case of the Inquiring Murderer is not simply an example I made up; it is Kant's own example. In an essay with the charmingly old-fashioned title "On a Supposed Right to Lie from Altruistic Motives," Kant discusses this case and gives a second argument for his view about it. He writes:

> After you have honestly answered the murderer's question as to whether his intended victim is at home, it may be that he has slipped out so that he does not come in the way of the murderer, and thus that the murder may not be committed. But if you had lied and said he was not at home when he had really gone out without your knowing it, and if the murderer had then met him as he went away and murdered him, you might justly be accused as the cause of his death. For if you had told the truth as far as you knew it, perhaps the murderer might have been apprehended by the neighbors while he searched the house and thus the deed might have been prevented. Therefore, whoever tells a lie, however well intentioned he might be, must answer for the consequences, however unforeseeable they were, and pay the penalty for them. . . .
>
> To be truthful (honest) in all deliberations, therefore, is a sacred and absolutely commanding decree of reason, limited by no expediency.

This argument may be stated in a more general form: We are tempted to make exceptions to the rule against lying because in some cases we think the consequences of truthfulness would be bad and the consequences of lying good. However, we can never be certain about what the consequences of our actions will be; we cannot *know* that good results will follow.

The results of lying *might* be unexpectedly bad. Therefore, the best policy is always to avoid the known evil—lying—and let the consequences come as they will. Even if the consequences are bad, they will not be our fault, for we will have done our duty.

The problems with this argument are obvious enough—so obvious, in fact, that it is surprising a philosopher of Kant's stature was not more sensitive to them. In the first place, the argument depends on an unreasonably pessimistic view of what we can know. Sometimes we can be quite confident of what the consequences of our actions will be, and justifiably so; in which case we need not hesitate because of uncertainty. Moreover—and this is a more interesting matter, from a philosophical point of view—Kant seems to assume that although we would be morally responsible for any bad consequences of lying, we would *not* be similarly responsible for any bad consequences of telling the truth. Suppose, as a result of our telling the truth, the murderer found his victim and killed him. Kant seems to assume that we would be blameless. But can we escape responsibility so easily? After all, we aided the murderer. This argument, then, like the first one, is not very convincing.

9.3. Conflicts Between Rules

The idea that moral rules are absolute, allowing no exceptions, is implausible in light of such cases as The Case of the Inquiring Murderer, and Kant's arguments for it are unsatisfactory. But are there any convincing arguments against the idea, apart from its being implausible?

The principal argument against absolute moral rules has to do with the possibility of conflict cases. Suppose it is held to be absolutely wrong to do A in any circumstances and also wrong to do B in any circumstances. Then what about the case in which a person is faced with the choice between doing A and doing B—when he must do something and there are no other alternatives available? This kind of conflict case seems to show that it is *logically* untenable to hold that moral rules are absolute.

Is there any way that this objection can be met? One way would be for the absolutist to deny that such cases ever actually occur. The British philosopher P. T. Geach takes just this view. Like Kant, Geach argues that moral rules are absolute; but his reasons are very different from Kant's. Geach holds that moral rules must be understood as absolute divine commands, and so he says simply that God will not allow conflict situations to arise. We can describe fictitious cases in which there is no way to avoid violating one of the absolute rules, but, he says, God will not permit such circumstances to exist in the real world. In his book *God and the Soul* (1969) Geach writes:

> "But suppose circumstances are such that observance of one Divine law, say the law against lying, involves breach of some other absolute Divine prohibition?"—If God is rational, he does not command the impossible; if God governs all events by his providence, he can see to it that circumstances in which a man is inculpably faced by a choice between forbidden acts do not occur. Of course such circumstances (with the clause "and there is no way out" written into their description) are consistently describable; but God's providence could ensure that they do not in fact arise. Contrary to what nonbelievers often say, belief in the existence of God does make a difference to what one expects to happen.

Do such circumstances ever actually arise? The Case of the Inquiring Murderer is, of course, a fictitious example; but it is not difficult to find real-life examples that make the same point. During the Second World War, Dutch fishermen regularly smuggled Jewish refugees to England in their boats, and the following sort of thing sometimes happened. A Dutch boat, with refugees in the hold, would be stopped by a Nazi patrol boat. The Nazi captain would call out and ask the Dutch captain where he was bound, who was on board, and so forth. The fishermen would lie and be allowed to pass. Now it is clear that the fishermen had only two alternatives, to lie or to allow their passengers (and themselves) to be taken and shot. No third alternative was available; they could not, for example, remain silent and outrun the Nazis.

Now suppose the two rules "It is wrong to lie" and "It is wrong to permit the murder of innocent people" are both taken to be absolute. The Dutch fishermen would have to do one of these things; therefore a moral view that absolutely prohibits both is incoherent. Of course this difficulty could be avoided if one held that only *one* of these rules is absolute; that would apparently be Kant's way out. But this dodge cannot work in every such case; so long as there are at least two "absolute rules," whatever they might be, the possibility will always exist that they might come into conflict. And that makes the view of those rules as absolute impossible to maintain.

9.4. Another Look at Kant's Basic Idea

Few philosophers would dispute Paton's statement that Kant's *Groundwork* "has exercised on human thought an influence almost ludicrously disproportionate to its size." Yet at the same time, few would defend The Categorical Imperative as Kant formulated it—as we have seen, it is beset by serious, perhaps insurmountable, problems. What, then, accounts for Kant's influence? Is there some basic idea underlying The Categorical Imperative that we might accept, even if we do not accept Kant's particular way of expressing it? I believe that there is, and that the power of this idea accounts, at least in part, for Kant's vast influence.

Remember that Kant thinks The Categorical Imperative is binding on rational agents simply because they are rational—in other words, a person who did not accept this principle would be guilty not merely of being immoral but of being *irrational*. This is a fascinating idea—that there are rational as well as moral constraints on what a good person may believe and do. But what exactly does this mean? In what sense would it be irrational to reject The Categorical Imperative?

The basic idea seems to be this: A moral judgment must be backed by good reasons—if it is true that you ought (or ought not) to do such-and-such, then there must be a *reason why* you should (or should not) do it. For example, you may think that you ought not to set forest fires because property would be destroyed and people would be killed. But if you accept those as reasons in *one* case, you must also accept them as reasons in *other* cases. It is no good saying that you accept those reasons some of the time, but not all the time; or that other people must respect them, but not you. Moral reasons, if they are valid at all, are binding on all people at all times. This is a requirement of consistency; and Kant was right to think that no rational person could deny it.

This is the Kantian idea—or, I should say, one of the Kantian ideas—that has been so influential. It has a number of important implications. It implies that a person cannot regard himself as special, from a moral point of view: he cannot consistently think that *he* is permitted to act in ways that are forbidden to others, or that *his* interests are more important than other people's interests. As one commentator remarked, I cannot say that it is all right for me to drink your beer and then complain when you drink mine. Moreover, it implies that there are *rational constraints* on what we may do: we may want to do something—say, drink someone else's beer—but recognize that we cannot *consistently* do it, because we cannot at the same time accept its implications. If Kant was not the first to recognize this, he was the first to make it the cornerstone of a fully worked-out system of morals. That was his great contribution.

But Kant went one step further and concluded that consistency requires rules that have no exceptions. It is not hard to see how his basic idea pushed him in that direction; but the extra step was not necessary, and it has caused trouble for his theory ever since. Rules, even within a Kantian framework, *need not* be regarded as absolute. All that is required by Kant's basic idea is that when we violate a rule, we do so for a reason that we would be willing for anyone to accept, were they in our position. In The Case of the Inquiring Murderer, this means that we may violate the rule against lying only if we would be willing for anyone to do so were he faced with the same situation. And *that* proposition causes little trouble.

CHAPTER 10

Kant and Respect for Persons

There is only one theory of punishment that is compatible with human dignity, and that is the theory of Kant.

KARL MARX, writing in the
NEW YORK DAILY TRIBUNE, February 18, 1853

10.1. The Idea of "Human Dignity"

The great German philosopher Immanuel Kant thought that human beings occupy a special place in creation. Of course he was not alone in thinking this. It is an old idea: from ancient times, humans have considered themselves to be essentially different from all other creatures—and not just different but *better.* In fact, humans have traditionally thought themselves to be quite fabulous. Kant certainly did. On his view, human beings have "an intrinsic worth, i.e., *dignity,*" which makes them valuable "above all price." Other animals, by contrast, have value only insofar as they serve human purposes. In his *Lectures on Ethics* (1779), Kant said:

> But so far as animals are concerned, we have no direct duties. Animals . . . are there merely as means to an end. That end is man.

We can, therefore, use animals in any way we please. We do not even have a "direct duty" to refrain from torturing them. Kant admits that it probably is wrong to torture them, but the reason is not that *they* would be hurt; the reason is only that *we* might suffer indirectly as a result of it, because "he who is cruel to animals becomes hard also in his dealings with men." Thus on Kant's view, mere animals have no moral importance at all. Human beings are, however, another story entirely. Ac-

127

cording to Kant, humans may never be "used" as means to an end. He even went so far as to suggest that this is the ultimate law of morality.

Like many other philosophers, Kant believed that morality can be summed up in one ultimate principle, from which all our duties and obligations are derived. He called this principle *The Categorical Imperative.* In the *Groundwork of the Metaphysics of Morals* (1785) he expressed it like this:

> Act only according to that maxim by which you can at the same time will that it should become a universal law.

However, Kant also gave *another* formulation of The Categorical Imperative. Later in the same book, he said that the ultimate moral principle may be understood as saying:

> Act so that you treat humanity, whether in your own person or in that of another, always as an end and never as a means only.

Scholars have wondered ever since why Kant thought these two rules were equivalent. They *seem* to express very different moral conceptions. Are they, as he apparently believed, two versions of the same basic idea, or are they really different ideas? We will not pause over this question. Instead we will concentrate here on Kant's belief that morality requires us to treat persons "always as an end and never as a means only." What exactly does this mean, and why did he think it true?

When Kant said that the value of human beings "is above all price," he did not intend this as mere rhetoric but as an objective judgment about the place of human beings in the scheme of things. There are two important facts about people that, in his view, support this judgment.

First, because people have desires and goals, other things have value *for them,* in relation to *their* projects. Mere "things" (and this includes nonhuman animals, whom Kant considered unable to have self-conscious desires and goals) have value only as means to ends, and it is human ends that *give* them value. Thus if you want to become a better chess player, a book of chess instruction will have value for you; but apart from such ends the book has no value. Or if you want to travel about, a car will have value for you; but apart from this desire the car will have no value.

Second, and even more important, humans have "an intrinsic worth, i.e., *dignity*," because they are *rational agents*—that is, free agents capable of making their own decisions, setting their own goals, and guiding their conduct by reason. Because the moral law is the law of reason, rational beings are the embodiment of the moral law itself. The only way that moral goodness can exist at all in the world is for rational creatures to apprehend what they should do and, acting from a sense of duty, do it. This, Kant thought, is the *only* thing that has "moral worth." Thus if there were no rational beings, the moral dimension of the world would simply disappear.

It makes no sense, therefore, to regard rational beings merely as one kind of valuable thing among others. They are the beings *for whom* mere "things" have value, and they are the beings whose conscientious actions have moral worth. So Kant concludes that their value must be absolute, and not comparable to the value of anything else.

If their value is "beyond all price," it follows that rational beings must be treated "always as an end, and never as a means only." This means, on the most superficial level, that we have a strict duty of beneficence toward other persons: we must strive to promote their welfare; we must respect their rights, avoid harming them, and generally "endeavor, so far as we can, to further the ends of others."

But Kant's idea also has a somewhat deeper implication. The beings we are talking about are *rational* beings, and "treating them as ends-in-themselves" means *respecting their rationality.* Thus we may never *manipulate* people, or *use* people, to achieve our purposes, no matter how good those purposes may be. Kant gives this example, which is similar to an example he uses to illustrate the first version of his categorical imperative: Suppose you need money, and so you want a "loan," but you know you will not be able to repay it. In desperation, you consider making a false promise (to repay) in order to trick a friend into giving you the money. May you do this? Perhaps you need the money for a good purpose—so good, in fact, that you might convince yourself the lie would be justified. Nevertheless, if you lied to your friend, you would merely be manipulating him and using him "as a means."

On the other hand, what would it be like to treat your friend "as an end"? Suppose you told the truth, that you need the money for a certain purpose but will not be able to repay it. Then your friend could make up his own mind about whether to let you have it. He could exercise his own powers of reason, consulting his own values and wishes, and make a free, autonomous choice. If he did decide to give the money for this purpose, he would be choosing to make that purpose *his own.* Thus you would not merely be using him as a means to achieving *your* goal. This is what Kant meant when he said, "Rational beings . . . must always be esteemed at the same time as ends, i.e., only as beings who must be able to contain in themselves the end of the very same action."

Now Kant's conception of human dignity is not easy to grasp; it is, in fact, probably the most difficult notion discussed in this book. We need to find a way to make the idea clearer. In order to do that, we will consider in some detail one of its most important applications—this may be better than a dry, theoretical discussion. Kant believed that if we take the idea of human dignity seriously, we will be able to understand the practice of criminal punishment in a new and revealing way. The rest of this chapter will be devoted to an examination of this example.

10.2. Retribution and Utility in the Theory of Punishment

Jeremy Bentham, the great utilitarian theorist, said that "all punishment is mischief: all punishment in itself is evil." By this he meant to point out that punishment always involves treating people badly, whether by taking away their freedom (imprisonment), their property (fines), or even their life (capital punishment). Since these things are all evils, they require justification. *Why* is it right to treat people like this?

The traditional answer is that punishment is justified as a way of "paying back" the offender for his evil deed. Those who have committed crimes, such as stealing from other people or assaulting other people, *deserve* to be treated badly in return. It is essentially a matter of justice: if someone harms other people, justice requires that he be harmed also. As the ancient saying has it, "An eye for an eye, a tooth for a tooth."

This view is known as *Retributivism*. Retributivism was, on Bentham's view, a wholly unsatisfactory idea, because it advocated the infliction of suffering without any compensating gain in happiness. Retributivism would have us *increase*, not decrease, the amount of suffering in the world. This is not a "hidden" implication of Retributivism. Kant, who was a retributivist, was aware of this implication and openly embraced it. In *The Critique of Practical Reason* (1788) he wrote:

> When someone who delights in annoying and vexing peace-loving folk receives at last a right good beating, it is certainly an ill, but everyone approves of it and considers it as good in itself *even if nothing further results from it.*

Thus punishing people may increase the amount of misery in the world; but according to Kant that is all right, for the extra suffering is borne by the criminal who, after all, deserves it.

Utilitarianism takes a very different approach. According to Utilitarianism, our duty is to do whatever will increase the amount of happiness in the world. Punishment is, on its face, "an evil" because it makes someone—the person who is punished—*un*happy. Thus Bentham says, "If it ought at all to be admitted, it ought to be admitted in as far as it promises to exclude some greater evil." In other words, it can be justified only if it will have good results that, on balance, outweigh the evil done.

So for the utilitarian, the question is: Does punishment have such good results? Is there a *good purpose* served by punishing criminals, other than simply making them suffer? Utilitarians have traditionally answered in the affirmative. There are two ways in which the practice of punishing lawbreakers benefits society.

First, punishing criminals helps to *prevent crime*, or at least to reduce the level of criminal activity in a society. People who are tempted to misbehave can be deterred from doing so if they know they will be punished. Of course, the threat of punishment will not *always* be efficacious. Sometimes people will break the law anyway. But there will be *less* misconduct if punishments are threatened. Imagine what it would be like if the police did not stand ready to arrest thieves; one would have to be a hopeless romantic not to recognize that there would be a lot more thievery. Since criminal misconduct causes unhappiness to its victims, in preventing crime (by providing for punishments) we are preventing unhappiness—in fact we are undoubtedly preventing *more* unhappiness than we are causing. Thus because there is a net gain in happiness, the utilitarian would see punishment as justified.

Second, a well-designed system of punishment might have the effect of *rehabilitating wrongdoers*. Without trying to excuse them, it must be admitted that criminals are often people with emotional problems, who find it difficult to function well in society. They are often ill educated and lack marketable skills. Considering this, why should we not respond to crime by attacking the problems that give rise to it? If a person is breaking society's rules, he is a danger to society and may first be imprisoned to remove the danger. But while he is there, his problems should be addressed—with psychological therapy, educational opportunities, or job training, as appropriate. If he can eventually be returned to society as a productive citizen, rather than as a criminal, both he and society will benefit.

The logical outcome of this way of thinking is that we should abandon the notion of *punishment* altogether, and replace it with the more humane notion of *treatment* for the criminal who so obviously needs it. Karl Menninger, the distinguished psychologist, expressed this conclusion when he wrote in 1959,

> We, the agents of society, must move to end the game of tit-for-tat and blow-for-blow in which the offender has foolishly engaged himself and us. We are not driven, as he is, to wild and impulsive actions. With knowledge comes power, and with power there is no need for the frightened vengeance of the old penology. In its place should go a quiet, dignified, therapeutic program for the rehabilitation of the disorganized one, if possible, the protection of society during the treatment period, and his guided return to useful citizenship, as soon as this can be effected.

These utilitarian ideas have dominated Anglo-American law for the past century; today the utilitarian theory of punishment is the reigning orthodoxy. Prisons, once mere places of confinement, have been redesigned (in theory, at least) as centers for rehabilitation, complete with psychologists, libraries, educational programs, and vocational training. The shift in thinking has been so great that the term "prison" is no longer in favor; in many places the preferred nomenclature is "correctional facility." Notice the implications of the new term—inmates are there not to be "punished" but to be "corrected." Of course, in many instances, the programs of rehabilitation have been dismally unsuccessful. Nevertheless, the programs are *designed* as rehabilitation. The victory of the utilitarian ideology has been virtually complete.

10.3. Kant's Retributivism

Like all orthodoxies, the utilitarian theory of punishment has generated opposition. Much of the opposition is practical in nature; the programs of rehabilitation, despite all the efforts that have been put into them, have not worked very well. In California, for example, more has been done to "rehabilitate" criminals than anywhere else; yet the rate of recidivism is higher there than in most other states. But some of the opposition is also based on purely theoretical considerations that go back at least to Kant.

Kant abjured "the serpent-windings of Utilitarianism" because, he said, the theory is incompatible with human dignity. In the first place, it has us calculating how to use people as means to an end, and this (he says) is morally impermissible. If we imprison the criminal in order to secure the well-being of society, we are merely *using* him for the benefit of others. This violates the fundamental rule that "one man ought never to be dealt with merely as a means subservient to the purpose of another."

Moreover, the aim of "rehabilitation," although it sounds noble enough, is actually no more than the attempt to mold people into what *we* think they should be. As such, it is a violation of their rights as autonomous beings, who are entitled to decide for themselves what sort of people they will be. We do have the right to respond to their wickedness by "paying them back" for it, but we do *not* have the right to violate their integrity by trying to manipulate their personalities.

Thus Kant would have no part of utilitarian justifications of punishment. Instead, he argued that punishment should be governed by two principles. First, people should be punished simply because they have committed crimes, and for no other reason:

> Juridical punishment can never be administered merely as a means for promoting another good either with regard to the criminal himself or to civil society, but must in all cases be imposed only because the individual on whom it is inflicted *has committed a crime*.

And second, Kant says it is important to punish the criminal *proportionately* to the seriousness of his crime. Small punishments may suffice for small crimes, but big punishments are necessary in response to big crimes:

> But what is the mode and measure of punishment which public justice takes as its principle and standard? It is just the principle of equality, by which the pointer of the scale of justice is made to incline no more to the one side than to the other. . . . Hence it may be said: "If you slander another, you slander yourself; if you steal from another, you steal from yourself; if you strike another, you strike yourself; if you kill another, you kill yourself." This is . . . the only principle which . . . can definitely assign both the quality and the quantity of a just penalty.

This second principle leads Kant inevitably to endorse capital punishment; for in response to murder, only death is a sufficiently stern penalty. In one of the most famous passages in Kant's writings, he says:

> Even if a civil society resolved to dissolve itself with the consent of all its members—as might be supposed in the case of a people inhabiting an island resolving to separate and scatter throughout the whole world—the last murderer lying in prison ought to be executed before the resolution was carried out. This ought to be done in

order that every one may realize the desert of his deeds, and that bloodguiltiness may not remain on the people; for otherwise they will all be regarded as participants in the murder as a public violation of justice.

It is worth noting that Utilitarianism has been faulted for violating both of Kant's principles. There is nothing in the basic idea of Utilitarianism that limits punishment to the guilty, or that limits the amount of punishment to the amount deserved. If the purpose of punishment is to secure the general welfare, as Utilitarianism says, it could sometimes happen that the general welfare will be served by "punishing" someone who has *not* committed a crime—an innocent person. Similarly, it might happen that the general welfare is promoted by punishing people excessively—a greater punishment might have a greater deterrent effect. But both of these are, on their face, violations of justice, which Retributivism would never allow.

Now Kant's two principles do not constitute an argument in favor of punishment or a justification of it. They merely describe limits on what punishment can justly involve: only the guilty may be punished, and the injury done to the person punished must be comparable to the injury he has inflicted on others. We still need an argument to show that the practice of punishment, conceived in this way, would be a morally good thing. We have already noted that Kant regards punishment as a matter of *justice*—he says that, if the guilty are not punished, justice is not done. This is one argument. But Kant also provides an additional argument, based on his conception of treating people as "ends in themselves." This additional argument is Kant's distinctive contribution to the theory of Retributivism.

On the face of it, it seems unlikely that we could describe punishing someone as "respecting him as a person" or as "treating him as an end-in-himself." How could taking away someone's freedom, by sending him to prison, be a way of "respecting" him? Yet that is exactly what Kant suggests. Even more paradoxically, he implies that *executing* someone may also be a way of treating him "as an end." How can this be?

Remember that, for Kant, treating someone as an "end-in-himself" means treating him *as a rational being*. Thus we have to ask, What does it mean to treat someone as a rational being? Now a rational being is someone who is capable of reasoning about his conduct and who freely decides what he will do, on the basis of his own rational conception of what is best. Because he has these capacities, a rational being is *responsible* for his actions. We need to bear in mind the difference between:

1. Treating someone as a responsible being

and

2. Treating someone as a being who is not responsible for his conduct.

Mere animals, who lack reason, are not responsible for their actions; nor are people who are mentally "sick" and not in control of themselves. In such cases it would be absurd to try to "hold them accountable." We could not properly feel gratitude or resentment toward them, for they are not responsible for any good or ill they cause. Moreover, we cannot expect them to understand why we treat them as we do, any more than they understand why they behave as they do. So we have no choice but to deal with them by manipulating them, rather than by addressing them as autonomous individuals. When we spank a dog who has urinated on the rug, for example, we may do so in an attempt to prevent him from doing it again— but we are merely trying to "train" him. We could not reason with him even if we wanted to. The same goes for mentally "sick" humans.

On the other hand, rational beings are responsible for their behavior and so may properly be "held accountable" for what they do. We may feel gratitude when they behave well, and resentment when they behave badly. Reward and punishment—not "training" or other manipulation—are the natural expression of this gratitude and resentment. Thus in punishing people, we are *holding them responsible* for their actions, in a way in which we cannot hold mere animals responsible. We are responding to them not as people who are "sick" or who have no control over themselves, but as people who have freely chosen their evil deeds.

Furthermore, in dealing with responsible agents, we may properly allow *their conduct* to determine, at least in part, how we respond to them. If someone has been kind to you, you may respond by being generous in return; and if someone is nasty to you, you may also take that into account in deciding how to deal with him or her. And why shouldn't you? Why should you treat everyone alike, regardless of how *they* have chosen to behave?

Kant gives this last point a distinctive twist. There is, on his view, a deep logical reason for responding to other people "in kind." The first formulation of The Categorical Imperative comes into play here. When we decide what to do, we in effect proclaim our wish that our conduct be made into a "universal law." Therefore, when a rational being decides to treat people in a certain way, he decrees that in his judgment *this is the way people are to be treated.* Thus if we treat him the same way in return, we are doing nothing more than treating him as *he has decided* people are to be treated. If he treats others badly, and we treat him badly, we are complying with his own decision. (Of course, if he treats others well, and we treat him well in return, we are also complying with the choice he has made.) We are allowing *him* to decide how he is to be treated—and so we are, in a perfectly clear sense, respecting his judgment, by allowing it to control our treatment of him. Thus Kant says of the criminal, "His own evil deed draws the punishment upon himself."

By associating punishment with the idea of treating people as rational beings, Kant gave the retributive theory a new depth. What we ultimately think of the theory will depend on what we think about the big issues Kant has identified—on what we judge the nature of crime, and the nature of criminals, to be. If lawbreakers are, as Menninger suggests, "disorganized personalities" who are "driven to wild and impulsive actions" over which they have no control, then the therapeutic model will inevitably have greater appeal than Kant's sterner attitude. In fact, Kant himself would have to agree that if they are *not* responsible agents, it would make no sense to resent their behavior and "punish" them for it. But to the extent that criminals are regarded as responsible people, without excuse, who simply choose to violate the rights of others for no rationally acceptable motive, Kantian retributivism will continue to have great persuasive power. In my concluding chapter—my sketch of a fully satisfactory moral theory—I draw on Kant's idea of respect for persons and on his retributivism.

CHAPTER 11

The Idea of a Social Contract

The passions that incline men to peace, are fear of death; desire of such things as are necessary to commodious living; and a hope by their industry to obtain them. And reason suggesteth convenient articles of peace, upon which men may be drawn to agreement. These articles, are they, which otherwise are called the Laws of Nature.

THOMAS HOBBES, *LEVIATHAN* (1651)

11.1. Hobbes's Argument

From ancient times it has been observed that human beings are social creatures: we are not hermits; we naturally live together in groups, wanting and needing the company of others of our own kind. Some philosophers have thought that this fact is the key to understanding morality. Morality, they say, arises when people are brought to accept the rules that are necessary for social living.

The line of reasoning that leads to this conclusion begins by asking what it would be like if there were no social rules and no commonly accepted mechanism for enforcing them. Imagine, if you will, that there were no such thing as government—no laws, no police, and no courts. In this situation, each of us would be free to do as we pleased; there would be no one to tell us we couldn't do this or that. We might call this *the state of nature*. What would it be like?

Thomas Hobbes, the foremost British philosopher of the seventeenth century, thought it would be dreadful. In the *Leviathan* he wrote that there would be

> no place for industry, because the fruit thereof is uncertain: and consequently no culture of the earth; no naviga-

tion, nor use of the commodities that may be imported by sea; no commodious building; no instruments of moving, and removing, such things as require much force; no knowledge of the face of the earth; no account of time; no arts; no letters; no society; and which is worst of all, continual fear, and danger of violent death; and the life of man, solitary, poor, nasty, brutish, and short.

Why would things be so bad? It is not because people are bad. Rather, it is because of certain basic facts about the conditions of human life. Hobbes appeals to four such facts in arguing that the state of nature would be intolerable:

1. First, there is the fact of *equality of need*. Each of us needs the same basic things in order to survive—food, clothing, shelter. Although we may differ in some of our needs (diabetics need insulin, others don't), we are all essentially very much alike.

2. Second, there is the fact of *scarcity*. We do not live in the Garden of Eden, where milk flows in streams and every tree hangs heavy with fruit. The world is a hard, inhospitable place, where the things we need to survive do not exist in plentiful supply. We have to work hard to produce them, and even then there often is not enough to go around.

3. If there are not enough essential goods to go around, who will get them? Since each of us wants to live, and to live as well as possible, each of us will want as much as we can get. But will we be able to prevail over the others, who also want the scarce goods? Hobbes thinks not, because of the third fact about our condition, the fact of *the essential equality of human power*. No one is so superior to everyone else, in strength and cunning, that he or she can prevail over them indefinitely. Of course, some people are smarter and stronger than others; but even the strongest can be brought down by several others acting in concert.

4. If we cannot prevail by our own strength, what hope do we have? Can we, for example, rely on the charity or good will of other people to help us? We cannot. The fourth and final fact is the fact of *limited altruism*. Even if people are not wholly selfish, they nevertheless care very much about themselves; and you cannot simply assume that whenever your vital interests conflict with their vital interests, they will step aside.

When we put these four facts together, a grim picture emerges. We all need the same basic things, and there aren't enough of them to go around. Therefore, we will be in a kind of competition for them. But no one has what it takes to prevail in this competition, and no one—or almost no one—will be willing to forgo the satisfaction of *his* needs in favor of others. The result, as Hobbes puts it, is a "constant state of war, of one with all." And it is a war no one can hope to win. The reasonable person who wants to survive will try to seize what he needs and prepare to defend it from attack. But others will be doing the same thing. This is why life in the state of nature would be intolerable.

Hobbes did not think this a mere speculation. He pointed out that this is what actually happens when governments collapse, as during a civil insurrection. People begin desperately to hoard food, arm themselves, and lock out their neighbors. (What would *you* do if tomorrow morning you woke up to discover that because of some great catastrophe the government had collapsed, so that there were no functioning laws, police, or courts?) Moreover, the nations of the world, without any meaningful international law, exist in relation to one another very much like individuals in the "state of nature," and they are constantly at one another's throats, armed and distrustful.

Clearly, what is needed to escape the state of nature is some way for people to cooperate with one another. By cooperating, and dividing the labor, the amount of essential goods could be increased and distributed to all who need them. But two things are required for this to happen. First, there must be guarantees that people will not harm one another—people must be able to work together without fear of attack, theft, or treachery. And second, people must be able to rely on one another to keep their agreements. If one person grows food and another spends his time ministering to the sick while still another builds houses—with each expecting to share in the benefits created by the others—each person in the chain must be able *to count on* the others to perform as expected.

Once these assurances are in place, a society can develop in which everyone is better off than they were in the state of nature. There can then be "commodities imported by the sea, commodious building, arts, letters," and the like. But—and this is one of Hobbes's main points—in order for this to happen, government must be established; for it is government, with its system of laws, police, and courts, that *ensures* that people can live with a minimum fear of attack and that people will have to keep their bargains with one another. Government is an indispensable part of the scheme.

To escape the state of nature, then, people must agree to the establishment of rules to govern their relations with one another, and they must agree to the establishment of an agency—the state—with the power necessary to enforce those rules. According to Hobbes, such an agreement actually exists, and that is what makes social living possible. This agreement, to which every citizen is a party, is called *the social contract.*

In addition to explaining the purpose of the state, The Social Contract Theory also explains the nature of morality. The two are closely linked: the state exists to enforce the most important rules necessary for social living, while morality *consists in* the whole set of rules that enhance social living.

Moreover, it is only within the context of the social contract that we can become moral agents, because the contract creates the conditions under which we can *afford* to care about others. In the state of nature, it is every man for himself; it would be foolish for anyone to adopt the policy of "looking out for others," because one could do so only at the cost of putting one's own interests in continual jeopardy. But in society, altruism becomes possible. By releasing us from "the continual fear of violent death," the social contract frees us to take heed of others. Jean Jacques Rousseau

(1712–1778), the French thinker who after Hobbes is most closely identified with this theory, went so far as to say that we become *different kinds of creatures* when we enter civilized relations with others. In his most famous work, *The Social Contract* (1762), Rousseau wrote:

> The passage from the state of nature to the civil state produces a very remarkable change in man. . . . Then only, when the voice of duty takes the place of physical impulses and right to appetite, does man, who so far had considered only himself, find that he is forced to act on different principles, and to consult his reason before listening to his inclinations. . . . His faculties are so stimulated and developed, his ideas so extended, his feelings so ennobled, and his whole soul so uplifted, that, did not the abuses of this new condition often degrade him below that which he left, he would be bound to bless continually the happy moment which took him from it forever, and, instead of a stupid and unimaginative animal, made him an intelligent being and a man.

And what does the "voice of duty" require this new man to do? It requires him to set aside his private, self-centered "inclinations" in favor of rules that impartially promote the welfare of everyone alike. But he is able to do this only because others have agreed to do the same thing—that is the essence of the "contract." Thus we can summarize the social contract conception of morality as follows:

Morality consists in the set of rules, governing how people are to treat one another, that rational people will agree to accept, for their mutual benefit, on the condition that others follow those rules as well.

11.2. The Prisoner's Dilemma

Hobbes's argument is one way of arriving at The Social Contract Theory. There is another line of thought, however, that has also impressed many philosophers in recent years. This line of thought is connected with a problem in decision theory known as *The Prisoner's Dilemma*. The Prisoner's Dilemma may be stated first in the form of a puzzle; you may want to see if you can solve it before looking at the answer.

Suppose you live in a totalitarian society, and one day, to

your astonishment, you are arrested and charged with treason. The police say that you have been plotting against the government with a man named Smith, who has also been arrested and is being held in a separate cell. The interrogator demands that you confess. You protest your innocence; you say that you don't even know Smith. But this does no good. It soon becomes clear your captors are not interested in the truth—you are going to be sent to prison no matter what. But the length of your sentence will depend on whether you confess. You are given the following information:

- If you confess and Smith does not, you will get one year in prison and Smith will get ten. (*You get one year—this is the best you can hope for.*)
- If neither of you confesses, you will each be sentenced to two years in prison. (*You get two years—this is second best.*)
- If you both confess, you will each be sentenced to five years in prison. (*You get five years—this is third best.*)
- If Smith confesses and you do not, you will get the ten years and he will get only one. (*You get ten years—this is the worst thing that could happen to you.*)

Finally, you are told that Smith is being offered the same deal; but you cannot communicate with him and you have no way of knowing what he will do.

The problem is this: assuming that your only goal is to protect your own interests, what should you do? Confess, or not confess? For the purposes of this problem, you should forget about maintaining your dignity, standing up for your rights, and other such notions. That is not what this problem is about. You should also forget about trying to help Smith. This problem is strictly about calculating what is in your own interests. The question is: what will get *you* the shortest sentence? Confessing or not confessing?

And now the answer: At first glance it may seem that the question cannot be answered unless you know what Smith will do. But that is an illusion. Actually, the problem has a perfectly clear solution: no matter what Smith does, you should confess. This can be shown by the following reasoning.

(1) Either Smith will confess or he won't.

(2) Suppose Smith confesses. Then, if you confess you will get five years, whereas if you do not confess you will get ten. Therefore, if he confesses, you are better off confessing as well.

(3) But suppose Smith does *not* confess. Then you are in this position: if you confess you will get one year, whereas if you do not confess you will get two. Clearly, then, even if Smith does not confess you will still be better off if you do.

(4) Therefore, you must confess. That is what will get you the shortest sentence, regardless of what Smith does.

So far, so good. But there is a catch. Remember that Smith is being offered the same deal. Assuming that he is not stupid, he will also conclude from the very same reasoning that *he* should confess. Thus the outcome will be that you will both confess, and this means that you will both be given five-year sentences. *But if you had both done the opposite, each of you would have gotten only two years.* That's the catch. By rationally pursuing your own interests, you both end up worse off than if you had acted differently. That is what makes the Prisoner's Dilemma a dilemma. It is a paradoxical situation: you will both be better off if you simultaneously do what is *not* in your own individual self-interests.

If you could communicate with Smith, of course, you could make an agreement with him. You could agree that neither of you would confess; then you could both get the shorter two-year sentence. By cooperating you would both be better off than if you acted independently. Cooperating will not get either of you the *optimum* result—the one-year sentence—but it will get both of you a better result than either of you could obtain if you did not cooperate.

It would be vital, however, that any agreement between you be enforceable, because if he reneged and confessed, while you kept the bargain and did not, then you would end up serving the maximum ten years while he served only one. Thus, in order for it to be rational for you to keep your part of such a bargain, you would have to be assured that he will have to keep his part. (And of course he would have the same worry about you reneging.) Only an enforceable agreement could provide a way out of the dilemma, for either of you.

Morality as the Solution to a Prisoner's-Dilemma-Type Problem. The Prisoner's Dilemma is not just a clever puzzle. Although the story we have told is fictitious, the pattern it exemplifies comes up often in real life. Prisoner's-Dilemma-type situations occur when two conditions are present:

1. It must be a situation in which people's interests are affected not only by what they do but by what other people do as well;

and

2. It must be a situation in which, paradoxically, everyone will end up worse off if they individually pursue their own interests than if they simultaneously do what is not in their own individual interests.

And this, it may be argued, is the kind of situation that each of us constantly faces when we try to pursue our own interests in the context of human society. The argument goes as follows.

In living together with other people, you could adopt either of two strategies. First, you could pursue your own self-interests exclusively—in every situation, you could do whatever will benefit yourself, taking no notice of how others might be affected. Let us call this "acting egoistically." Alternatively, you could be concerned with other people's welfare as well as your own, balancing the two against one another, and sometimes forgoing your own interests in order to benefit them. Let us call this strategy "acting benevolently."

But it is not only you who has to make this decision. Other people will also have to decide which policy to adopt. There are four possibilities: first, you could be an egoist while other people are benevolent; second, others could be egoists while you are benevolent; third, everyone could be egoistic; and fourth, everyone could be benevolent. You must consider how you would fare in each of these situations. Purely from the point of view of advancing your own welfare, you might assess the possibilities like this:

- You would be best off in a situation in which you were an egoist while other people were benevolent. Other people would faithfully respect your interests, but you would be free to ignore theirs whenever it was to your advantage to do so. (In this situation you would be, in the terminology of decision theory, a "free rider.")
- The next best situation for you would be one in which everyone was benevolent. You would no longer have the advantage of being able to ignore other people's interests, but at least you would have the advantages that go with considerate treatment by others. (This is the situation of ordinary "morality.")
- A bad situation, but not the worst, would be one in which everyone was egoistic. You would try to protect your own interests, although you would get little help from anyone else. (This is Hobbes's "state of nature.")
- And finally, you would be *worst* off in a situation in which you respect other people's interests but they ignore yours. Other people could knife you in the back when it was to their advantage, but you would not be free to do the same. You would come out on the short end every time. (Making up our own terminology, we might say that in this situation you are a "sucker.")

Now this is exactly the kind of array that gives rise to the Prisoner's Dilemma. Based on these assessments, you should conclude that you should *not* adopt the policy of respecting other people's interests:

   (1) Either other people will respect your interests or they won't.

   (2) If they do respect your interests, you will be better off not respecting theirs, at least whenever it is to

your advantage not to do so. This will be the optimum situation.

(3) If they do not respect your interests, then it would be foolish for you to respect theirs—that would land you in the worst possible situation.

(4) Therefore, regardless of what other people do, you are better off adopting the policy of not respecting their interests, at least when it would be to your own advantage.

And now we come to the catch: other people, of course, can reason in the same way, and the result will be that we end up back in Hobbes's state of nature, with everyone willing to knife everyone else whenever they see some advantage in it for themselves. *And in this situation each of us is obviously worse off than we would be if we cooperated.* To escape the dilemma, we need another enforceable agreement, this time an agreement to obey the rules of mutually respectful social living. As before, cooperation would not yield the optimum outcome (us being egoists while others are benevolent), but it would lead to a better result than could be obtained by each of us independently pursuing our own interests. We need, in David Gauthier's words, to "bargain our way into morality." We can do that if we can establish sufficient sanctions to ensure that, if we respect other people's interests, they must respect ours as well.

11.3. Some Advantages of The Social Contract Theory of Morals

The Social Contract Theory of Morals is, as we have said, the idea that *Morality consists in the set of rules, governing how people are to treat one another, that rational people will agree to accept, for their mutual benefit, on the condition that others follow those rules as well.*

The strength of The Social Contract Theory of Morals (hereafter, for brevity, I will simply say "The Social Contract Theory") is due, in large measure, to the fact that it provides simple and plausible answers to the difficult questions about morality that have always perplexed philosophers. Let us look at a few of those questions.

1. *What moral rules are we bound to follow, and how are those rules justified?* The key idea is that morally binding rules are the ones that are necessary for social living. It is obvious, for example, that we could not live together very well if we did not accept rules prohibiting murder, assault, theft, lying, breaking promises, and the like. These rules are justified simply by showing that they are necessary if we are to cooperate for our mutual benefit. On the other hand, *some* rules that are often suggested as moral rules—such as the prohibition of prostitution, pornography, and sexual promiscuity—are not obviously justifiable in this way. (How is social living threatened by one person's engaging in voluntary private sexual activity with another? If this conduct does not threaten us in any way, then it is outside the scope of the social contract and is none of our business.) Those rules, therefore, have only a doubtful claim on us.

2. *Why is it reasonable for us to follow the moral rules?* We agree to follow the moral rules because it is to our own advantage to live in a society in which the rules are accepted. Of course, it may sometimes be to our short-term benefit to break the rules. However, it is not reasonable for us to want an arrangement in which people violate the rules any time it is advantageous for them to do so—the whole point of the social contract is that we want to be able to *count on* people to keep the rules, except perhaps in the most dire emergencies. Only then can we feel safe. Therefore, our own steady compliance is the reasonable price we pay in order to secure the steady compliance of others.

3. *Under what circumstances are we allowed to break the rules?* This is a somewhat more complicated matter. The key idea here is the idea of *reciprocity*—we agree to obey the rules on the condition that others obey them as well. Thus when someone violates the condition of reciprocity, he releases us, at least to some extent, from our obligation toward him. Suppose someone refuses to be helpful to you, in circumstances in which he clearly should help you. Then, if later on he needs *your* help, you may rightly feel that you have less of a duty to help him.

The same basic point explains why it is permissible to punish those who have broken the criminal law. Lawbreakers are treated differently from normal citizens—in punishing them, we treat them in ways that are not normally permitted. How can this be justified? The answer has two parts. In the first place, the purpose of the state is to *enforce* the primary rules necessary for social living. If we are to live together without fear, it cannot be left up to the individual's discretion whether he or she will attack others, steal from them, and so forth. Attaching sanctions to the violation of these rules is the only workable means of enforcing them. It follows that we *need* to punish. But why is it *permissible* to punish? The answer is that the criminal has violated the fundamental condition of reciprocity: we recognize the rules of social living as limiting what *we* can do only on the condition that others accept the same restrictions on what *they* can do. Therefore, by violating the rules with respect to us, criminals release us from our obligation toward them and leave themselves open to retaliation.

Finally, there is an even more dramatic circumstance in which one may violate the moral rules. In normal circumstances, morality requires that one be *impartial,* that is, that one give no greater weight to one's own interests than to the interests of others. But suppose you face a situation in which you must choose between your own death and the deaths of five other people. Impartiality, it seems, would require you to choose your own death; after all, there are five of them and only one of you. Are you morally bound to sacrifice yourself?

Philosophers have often felt uneasy about this sort of case; they have felt instinctively that somehow there are limits to what morality can demand of us. Therefore they have traditionally said that such heroic actions are *supererogatory*—that is, they are actions above and beyond the call of duty—admirable when they occur, but not strictly required. Yet it is hard to explain why such actions are not strictly required. If morality demands impartial decisions, and impartial reason decrees it is better for one to die than five, why is one not required to sacrifice oneself?

The Social Contract Theory has an explanation. It is rational to accept the social contract because doing so is to our own advantage; by accepting it, we escape the state of nature.

We give up our unconditional freedom, but in return we get the advantages of social living. However, if we are then required by the contract to give up our lives, we are no better off than we were in the state of nature; and so we no longer have any reason to abide by the contract. Thus there is a natural limit on the amount of self-sacrifice that can be expected from anyone: we may not exact a sacrifice so profound that it negates the very point of the contract. In this way The Social Contract Theory explains a feature of morality that on other theories remains mysterious.

4. *Are there moral "facts"? Does morality have an objective basis? Are moral judgments objectively true?* Philosophers have long wondered whether our moral opinions represent anything more than our subjective feelings or the customs of our society. They have felt that there must be *something* more to morality than customs and feelings, but it is hard to say just what that something is. If there are moral "facts," what kind of thing could they be?

One of the main attractions of The Social Contract Theory is that it sweeps aside all these worries so easily. No long explanation is needed. Morality is not merely a matter of customs or feelings; it has an objective basis. But the theory does not need to postulate any special kinds of "facts" to explain that basis. Morality is the set of rules that rational people would agree to accept for their mutual benefit. We can determine what those rules are by rational investigation and then determine whether a particular act is morally acceptable by seeing whether it conforms to the rules. Once this is understood, the old worries about moral "objectivity" simply vanish.

11.4. The Problem of Civil Disobedience

Moral theories should provide help in understanding particular moral issues. The Social Contract Theory is based on an important insight about the nature of society and its institutions, and so it is especially well suited to helping us deal with issues involving those institutions. As a result of the social contract, we have an obligation to obey the law. But are we ever justified in *defying* the law? And if so, when?

The classic modern examples of civil disobedience are,

of course, the actions taken in connection with the Indian in-
dependence movement led by Gandhi and the American civil
rights movement led by Martin Luther King, Jr. Both move-
ments were characterized by public, conscientious, nonviolent
refusal to comply with the law. But the goals of the move-
ments were importantly different. Gandhi and his followers
did not recognize the right of the British to govern India; they
wanted to replace British rule with an entirely different system. King and his followers, on the other hand, did not question the legitimacy of the basic institutions of American government. They objected only to particular laws and social
policies that they regarded as unjust—so unjust, in fact, that
extreme measures were advocated as a means of challenging
them.

In his *Letter from the Birmingham City Jail* (1963), King detailed the frustration and anger that arises

> when you have seen vicious mobs lynch your mothers
> and fathers at will and drown your sisters and brothers at
> whim; when you have seen hate-filled policemen curse,
> kick, brutalize and even kill your black brothers and sis-
> ters with impunity; when you see the vast majority of your
> twenty million Negro brothers smothering in an air-tight
> cage of poverty in the midst of an affluent society; when
> you suddenly find your tongue twisted and your speech
> stammering as you seek to explain to your six-year-old
> daughter why she can't go to the public amusement park
> that has just been advertised on television, and see tears
> welling up in her little eyes when she is told that Funtown
> is closed to colored children, and see the depressing
> clouds of inferiority begin to distort her little personality.

The problem was not only that racial segregation, with all its
attendant evils, was enforced by social custom; it was a matter
of *law* as well, a law that black citizens were denied a voice in
formulating. When urged to rely on ordinary democratic pro-
cesses to redress his grievances, King first pointed out that
there had been many attempts at progress by negotiation, but
these efforts had met with little success; and as for "democ-
racy," the word had little meaning to Southern blacks:
"Throughout the state of Alabama all types of conniving

methods are used to prevent Negroes from becoming registered voters and there are some counties without a single
Negro registered to vote despite the fact that the Negro con-
stitutes a majority of the population."

King believed, therefore, that blacks had no choice but
to put their case before the public by defying the unjust laws.
Today, with King acclaimed as one of the giants of our time,
and with the civil rights movement remembered as a great
moral crusade, it takes an effort to recall how controversial
the strategy of civil disobedience was. Many liberals, while expressing sympathy for the goals of the movement, nevertheless denied that disobeying the law was a legitimate means of
pursuing those goals. An article published in the *New York
State Bar Journal* in 1965 expressed the typical worries. After as-
suring his readers that "long before Dr. King was born, I es-
poused, and still espouse, the cause of civil rights for all people," Louis Waldman, a prominent New York lawyer, argued:

> Those who assert rights under the Constitution and the
> laws made thereunder must abide by that Constitution
> and the law, if that Constitution is to survive. They can-
> not pick and choose; they cannot say they will abide by
> those laws which they think are just and refuse to abide
> by those laws which they think are unjust. . . .
>
> The country, therefore, cannot accept Dr. King's
> doctrine that he and his followers will pick and choose,
> knowing that it is illegal to do so. I say, such doctrine is
> not only illegal and for that reason alone should be aban-
> doned, but that it is also immoral, destructive of the prin-
> ciples of democratic government, and a danger to the
> very civil rights Dr. King seeks to promote.

Waldman was surely right to this extent: violating the law,
and claiming to be *justified* in doing so, is on its face a bad
thing, especially if the legal system is basically decent, because
such defiance may very well tend to weaken respect for the
values which the law protects. To meet this objection, those
who advocate civil disobedience need an argument to show
why their defiance of the law is justified. One such argument,
which King often used, is that the evils being opposed (the
evils of racial segregation) are so serious, so numerous, and so

resistant to remedy by less drastic means, that civil disobedience is justified as a "last resort." The end justifies the means,
even though the means are somewhat objectionable. This, in
the opinion of many moralists, is a perfectly sufficient reply to
the point made by Waldman. But there is a more profound
reply available, one suggested by The Social Contract Theory.

Why do we have an obligation to obey the law in the first
place? According to The Social Contract Theory, it is because
each of us participates in a complicated arrangement whereby
we gain certain benefits in return for accepting certain burdens. The benefits are the benefits of social living: we escape
the state of nature, and live in a society in which we are secure
and enjoy basic rights under the law. In order to gain these
benefits, we agree that we will do our part to uphold the institutions that make them possible. This means that we must
obey the law, pay our taxes, and so forth—these are the burdens we accept in return.

But what if things are arranged so that one group of people within the society is *not* accorded the rights enjoyed by
others? What if, instead of protecting them, "hate-filled po-
licemen curse, kick, brutalize and even kill . . . with im-
punity"? What if they are "smothered in an air-tight cage of
poverty" by being denied the opportunity to acquire decent
education or decent jobs? If the denial of these rights is sufficiently widespread and sufficiently systematic, we are forced to
conclude that *the terms of the social contract are not being honored*.
Thus if we continue to demand that the disadvantaged group
obey the law and otherwise respect society's institutions, *we are
demanding that they accept the burdens imposed by the social arrangement even though they are denied its benefits*.

This line of reasoning suggests that, rather than civil disobedience being an undesirable "last resort" for socially disenfranchised groups, it is in fact the most natural and reasonable means of expressing protest. For when they are denied a
fair share of the benefits of social living, the disenfranchised
are in effect released from the contract that otherwise would
require them to support the arrangements that make those
benefits possible. This is the deepest reason that justifies civil
disobedience, and it is to the credit of The Social Contract
Theory that it exposes this point so clearly.

11.5. Difficulties for the Theory

The Social Contract Theory has not had a large number of advocates among philosophers, although recently there have been some signs of change in this regard. Most thinkers have been attracted to other views instead. It is not clear why this should be so; the theory has a number of attractive features, as we have noted, and the arguments against it, although powerful, are no more impressive than the objections that have been directed at other, more popular views. What can be said against the theory? The following two objections seem to have the greatest weight.

1. The most common objection to the theory has been that it is based on a historical fiction. We are asked to imagine that people once lived in isolation from one another; that they found this intolerable; and that they eventually banded together, agreeing to follow social rules of mutual benefit. *But none of this ever happened.* It is just a fantasy. So of what relevance is it? To be sure, if people *had* come together in this way, we could explain their obligations to one another as the theory suggests: they would be obligated to obey the rules because they would have contracted to do so. But even then, there would still be trouble. We would have to face such questions as: Was the agreement unanimous? If not, what of the people who did not sign—are *they* not required to act morally? And if the contract was consummated a long time ago, are we supposed to be bound by the agreements of our ancestors? If not, how is the "contract" renewed in each new generation? But in fact there never was such a contract, and so nothing can sensibly be explained by appealing to it. As one critic of the theory wisecracked, the social contract "isn't worth the paper it's not written on."

To this criticism, the following reply might be offered. First, it might be urged that there is an *implicit* social contract by which we are all bound. To be sure, none of us ever actually signed a "real" contract—there is no document, with signatures affixed. However, there does exist a social arrangement very much like the one described in The Social Contract Theory: there is a set of rules that everyone recognizes as binding on them, and we all benefit from the fact that these rules are followed. Each of us accepts the benefits conferred by this arrangement; and more than that, we expect and encourage other people to continue observing the rules. This is a description of the actual state of affairs; it is not fictitious. By accepting the benefits of this arrangement, we incur an obligation to do our part in supporting it—in other words, to reciprocate. The contract is "implicit" because we become a part of it not through our words but through our actions.

Thus the story of the "social contract" need not be intended as a description of historical events. Rather, it is a useful analytical tool, based on the idea that we may understand our moral obligations *as if* they had arisen in this way. Consider the following situation. Suppose you were to come upon a group of people playing an elaborate game. It looks like fun, and so you join in. After a while, however, you begin to break some of the rules, because that looks like more fun. The others protest; they say that if you are going to play, you must follow the rules. You reply that you never promised to follow the rules. They may rightly reply that this is irrelevant. Perhaps *nobody* explicitly promised to obey; nevertheless, by joining the game, each person implicitly agrees to abide by the rules that make the game possible. It is *as though* they had all agreed. Morality is like this. The game is social living; we derive enormous benefits from it, and we do not want to forgo those benefits; but in order to play the game and get the benefits, we have to follow the rules.

It isn't clear to what extent the great social contract theorists, such as Hobbes and Rousseau, would accept this way of defending their view. But that doesn't matter; the reply seems to save the theory from what would otherwise be a devastating objection.

2. We have already observed that moral theories should provide help in dealing with practical moral issues. The important theories do this, but all too often a theory that clarifies one issue only confuses another—for each theory, there are some issues on which its pronouncements seem exactly right; but problems are caused when, on other issues, the theory's implications seem unacceptable. When we considered the problem of civil disobedience, The Social Contract Theory seemed to provide considerable insight. But in connec-

tion with some other issues, its implications are more disturbing.

The second objection to The Social Contract Theory, which seems to me more powerful than the first, has to do with its implications for our duties toward beings who are not able to participate in the contract. Nonhuman animals, for example, lack the capacities necessary to enter into any sort of agreements with us, whether explicit or implicit. Therefore it seems impossible that they should be covered by any "rules of mutual benefit" established by such an agreement. Nevertheless, isn't it morally wrong to torture an animal, when there is no good reason for it? And isn't this wrong *because of the pain caused to the animal itself?* But the idea of moral duties with respect to beings who are *outside* the contract seems contrary to the most basic idea behind the theory. Thus the theory seems to be defective.

Hobbes was aware that, on his view, animals are excluded from moral consideration. He wrote that "to make covenants with brute beasts, is impossible." Apparently this did not bother him. The other animals have never been treated well by humans, but in Hobbes's day animals were held in especially low regard. Descartes and Malebranche, two of Hobbes's contemporaries, had popularized the idea that, in addition to lacking souls, animals are not even capable of feeling pain. For Descartes, this was because animal bodies are mere machines; for Malebranche, it was necessary for the theological reason that all suffering is a consequence of Adam's sin, and animals are not descended from Adam. But regardless of the reason, the fashionable view was that because animals cannot suffer, they are necessarily beyond the reach of moral consideration. This enabled seventeenth-century scientists to experiment on animals with perfect indifference to their nonexistent "feelings." Nicholas Fontaine, an eyewitness, described these scientists at work in his memoirs, published in 1738:

> They administered beatings to dogs with perfect indifference, and made fun of those who pitied the creatures as if they felt pain. They said the animals were clocks; that the cries they emitted when struck were only the noise of a little spring that had been touched, but that the whole body was without feeling. They nailed poor animals up

on boards by their four paws to vivisect them and see the circulation of the blood which was a great subject of conversation.

If we do have a duty not to cause needless suffering to animals, it is difficult to see how that duty could be accommodated within The Social Contract Theory. However, many people, like Hobbes, might not find this so worrisome, for they might not regard the question of duties to mere animals as particularly urgent. But there is a further difficulty, of a similar kind, which may still give them pause.

Many humans are mentally retarded to such an extent that they cannot participate in the kind of agreements envisioned by The Social Contract Theory. They are certainly capable of suffering, and even of living a kind of rudimentary human life. But they are not sufficiently intelligent to understand the consequences of their actions or to know when they are hurting others, and so we may not rightly hold them responsible for their conduct. These humans pose exactly the same problem for the theory as nonhuman animals. Since they cannot participate in the agreements that, according to the theory, give rise to moral obligations, they are outside the realm of moral consideration. Yet we do think that we have moral obligations toward them. Moreover, our obligations toward them are often based on exactly the same reasons as our obligations toward normal humans—the primary reason we should not torture normal people, for example, is because it causes them terrible pain; and this is exactly the same reason we should not torture mentally retarded people. The Social Contract Theory can explain our duty in the case of normal people but not in the case of retarded people. Unless some way can be found to remedy this difficulty, the verdict must be that the basic idea of the theory is deeply flawed.

CHAPTER 12

The Ethics of Virtue

The concepts of obligation, and duty—*moral* obligation and *moral* duty, that is to say—and of what is *morally* right and wrong, and of the *moral* sense of "ought," ought to be jettisoned. . . . It would be a great improvement if, instead of "morally wrong," one always named a genus such as "untruthful," "unchaste," "unjust."

G. E. M. ANSCOMBE, *MODERN MORAL PHILOSOPHY* (1958)

12.1. The Ethics of Virtue and the Ethics of Right Action

In thinking about any subject it makes a great deal of difference what questions we begin with. In Aristotle's *Nicomachean Ethics* (ca. 325 B.C.), the central questions are about *character*. Aristotle begins by asking "What is the good of man?" and his answer is that "The good of man is an activity of the soul in conformity with virtue." To understand ethics, therefore, we must understand what makes someone a virtuous person, and Aristotle, with a keen eye for the details, devotes much space to discussing such particular virtues as courage, self-control, generosity, and truthfulness. The good man is the man of virtuous character, he says, and so the virtues are taken to be the subject-matter of ethics.

Although this way of thinking is closely identified with Aristotle, it was not unique to him—it was also the approach taken by Socrates, Plato, and a host of other ancient thinkers. They all approached the subject by asking: *What traits of character make one a good person?* and as a result "the virtues" occupied center stage in all of their discussions.

As time passed, however, this way of thinking about ethics came to be neglected. With the coming of Christianity a new set of ideas was introduced. The Christians, like the Jews, were monotheists who viewed God as a lawgiver, and for them righteous living meant obedience to the divine commandments. The Greeks had viewed reason as the source of practical wisdom—the virtuous life was, for them, inseparable from the life of reason. But St. Augustine, the fourth-century Christian thinker who was to be enormously influential, distrusted reason and taught that moral goodness depends on subordinating oneself to the will of God. Therefore, when the medieval philosophers discussed the virtues, it was in the context of Divine Law. The "theological virtues"—faith, hope, charity, and, of course, *obedience*—came to have a central place.

After the Renaissance, moral philosophy began to be secularized once again, but philosophers did not return to the Greek way of thinking. Instead, the Divine Law was replaced by its secular equivalent, something called the *Moral Law*. The Moral Law, which was said to spring from human reason rather than divine fiat, was conceived to be a system of rules specifying which actions are right. Our duty as moral agents, it was said, is to follow its directives. Thus modern moral philosophers approached their subject by asking a fundamentally different question than the one that had been asked by the ancients. Instead of asking: *What traits of character make one a good person?* they began by asking: *What is the right thing to do?* This led them in a different direction. They went on to develop theories, not of virtue, but of rightness and obligation:

- Each person ought to do whatever will best promote his or her own interests. (Ethical Egoism)
- We ought to do whatever will promote the greatest happiness for the greatest number. (Utilitarianism)
- Our duty is to follow rules that we could consistently will to be universal laws—that is, rules that we would be willing to have followed by all people in all circumstances. (Kant's theory)
- The right thing to do is to follow the rules that rational, self-interested people can agree to establish for their mutual benefit. (The Social Contract Theory)

And these are the familiar theories that have dominated modern moral philosophy from the seventeenth century on.

12.2. Should We Return to the Ethics of Virtue?

Recently a number of philosophers have advanced a radical idea: they have suggested that modern moral philosophy is bankrupt and that, in order to salvage the subject, we should return to Aristotle's way of thinking.

This idea was first put forth in 1958 when the distinguished British philosopher G. E. M. Anscombe published an article called "Modern Moral Philosophy" in the academic journal *Philosophy*. In that article she suggested that modern moral philosophy is misguided because it rests on the incoherent notion of a "law" without a lawgiver. The very concepts of obligation, duty, and rightness, on which modern moral philosophers have concentrated their attention, are inextricably linked to this nonsensical idea. Therefore, she concluded, we should stop thinking about obligation, duty, and rightness. We should abandon the whole project that modern philosophers have pursued and return instead to Aristotle's approach. This means that the concept of virtue should once again take center stage.

In the wake of Anscombe's article a flood of books and essays appeared discussing the virtues, and "virtue theory" soon became a major option in contemporary moral philosophy. There is, however, no settled body of doctrine on which all these philosophers agree. Compared to such theories as Utilitarianism, virtue theory is still in a relatively undeveloped state. Yet the virtue theorists are united in believing that modern moral philosophy has been on the wrong track and that a radical reorientation of the subject is needed.

In what follows we shall first take a look at what the theory of virtue is like. Then we shall consider some of the reasons that have been given for thinking that the ethics of virtue is superior to other, more modern ways of approaching the subject. And at the end we will consider whether a "return to the ethics of virtue" is really a viable option.

12.3. The Virtues

A theory of virtue should have several components. First, there should be an explanation of what a virtue *is*. Second, there should be a list specifying which character traits are virtues. Third, there should be an explanation of what these virtues consist in. Fourth, there should be an explanation of why these qualities are good ones for a person to have. Finally, the theory should tell us whether the virtues are the same for all people or whether they differ from person to person or from culture to culture.

What Is Virtue? The first question that must be asked is: *What is a virtue?* Aristotle suggested one possible answer. He said that a virtue is a trait of character that is manifested in habitual actions. The virtue of honesty is not possessed by someone who tells the truth only occasionally or whenever it is to his own advantage. The honest person is truthful as a matter of principle; his actions "spring from a firm and unchangeable character."

This is a start, but it is not enough. It does not distinguish virtues from vices, for vices are also traits of character manifested in habitual action. Edmund L. Pincoffs, a philosopher at the University of Texas, has made a suggestion that takes care of this problem. Pincoffs suggests that virtues and vices are qualities that we refer to in deciding whether someone is to be sought or avoided. "Some sorts of persons we prefer; others we avoid," he says. "The properties on our list [of virtues and vices] can serve as reasons for preference or avoidance."

We seek out people for different purposes, and this makes a difference to the virtues that are relevant. In looking for an auto mechanic, we want someone who is skillful, honest, and conscientious; in looking for a teacher, we want someone who is knowledgeable, articulate, and patient. Thus the virtues associated with auto repair are different from the virtues associated with teaching. But we also assess people *as people,* in a more general way: and so we have the concept, not just of a good mechanic or a good teacher, but of a good person. The moral virtues are the virtues of persons as such.

Taking our cue from Pincoffs, then, we may define a virtue as *a trait of character, manifested in habitual action, that it is good for a person to have.*

What Are the Virtues? What, then, *are* the virtues? Which traits of character should be fostered in human beings? There is no short answer, but the following is a partial list:

benevolence	fairness	reasonableness
civility	friendliness	self-confidence
compassion	generosity	self-control
conscientiousness	honesty	self-discipline
cooperativeness	industriousness	self-reliance
courage	justice	tactfulness
courteousness	loyalty	thoughtfulness
dependability	moderation	tolerance

The list could be expanded, of course, with other traits added. But this is a reasonable start.

What Do These Virtues Consist In? It is one thing to say, in a general way, that we should be conscientious and compassionate; it is another thing to try to say exactly what these character traits consist in. Each of the virtues has its own distinctive features and raises its own distinctive problems. There isn't enough space here to consider all the items on our list, but we may examine four of them briefly.

1. *Courage.* According to Aristotle, virtues are means poised between extremes; a virtue is "the mean by reference to two vices: the one of excess and the other of deficiency." Courage is a mean between the extremes of cowardice and foolhardiness—it is cowardly to run away from all danger; yet it is foolhardy to risk too much.

Courage is sometimes said to be a military virtue because it is so obviously needed to accomplish the soldier's task. Soldiers do battle; battles are fraught with danger; and so without courage the battle will be lost. But soldiers are not the only ones who need courage. Courage is needed by anyone who faces danger—and at different times this includes all of us. A scholar who spends his timid and safe life studying medieval literature might seem the very opposite of a soldier. Yet even he might become ill and need courage to face a dangerous operation. As Peter Geach (a contemporary British philosopher) puts it:

> Courage is what we all need in the end, and it is constantly needed in the ordinary course of life: by women who are with child, by all of us because our bodies are vulnerable, by coalminers and fishermen and steel-workers and lorry-drivers.

So long as we consider only "the ordinary course of life," the nature of courage seems unproblematic. But unusual circumstances present more troublesome types of cases. Consider a Nazi soldier, for example, who fights valiantly—he faces great risk without flinching—but he does so in an evil cause. Is he courageous? Geach holds that, contrary to appearances, the Nazi soldier does not really possess the virtue of courage at all. "Courage in an unworthy cause," he says, "is no virtue; still less is courage in an evil cause. Indeed I prefer not to call this non-virtuous facing of danger 'courage.' "

It is easy to see Geach's point. Calling the Nazi soldier "courageous" seems to praise his performance, and we should not want to praise it. Instead we would rather he behaved differently. Yet neither does it seem quite right to say that he is *not* courageous—after all, look at how he behaves in the face of danger. To get around this problem perhaps we should just say that he displays *two* qualities of character, one that is admirable (steadfastness in facing danger) and one that is not (a willingness to defend a despicable regime). He is courageous all right, and courage is an admirable thing; but because his courage is deployed in an evil cause, his behavior is *on the whole* wicked.

2. *Generosity.* Generosity is the willingness to expend one's resources to help others. Aristotle says that, like courage, it is also a mean between extremes: it stands somewhere between stinginess and extravagance. The stingy person gives too little, the extravagant person gives too much. But how much is enough?

The answer will depend to some extent on what general ethical view we accept. Jesus, another important ancient teacher, said that we must give all we have to help the poor. The possession of riches, while the poor starve, was in his view unacceptable. This was regarded by those who heard him as a hard teaching and it was generally rejected. It is still rejected by most people today, even by those who consider themselves to be his followers.

The modern utilitarians are, in this regard at least, Jesus' moral descendants. They hold that in every circumstance it is one's duty to do whatever will have the best overall consequences for everyone concerned. This means that we should be generous with our money until the point has been reached at which further giving would be more harmful to us than it would be helpful to others.

Why do people resist this idea? Partly it may be a matter of selfishness; we do not want to make ourselves poor by giving away what we have. But there is also the problem that adopting such a policy would prevent us from living normal lives. Not only money but time is involved. Our lives consist in projects and relationships that require a considerable investment of both. An ideal of "generosity" that demands spending our money and time as Jesus and the utilitarians recommend would require that we abandon our everyday lives and live very differently.

A reasonable interpretation of the demands of generosity might, therefore, be something like this: we should be as generous with our resources as is consistent with conducting our ordinary lives in a minimally satisfying way. Even this, though, will leave us with some awkward questions. Some people's "ordinary lives" are quite extravagant—think of a rich person whose everyday life includes luxuries without which he would feel deprived. The virtue of generosity, it would seem, cannot exist in the context of a life that is too sumptuous, especially when there are others about whose basic needs are unmet. To make this a "reasonable" interpretation of the demands of generosity, we need a conception of ordinary life that is itself not too extravagant.

3. *Honesty.* The honest person is, first of all, someone who does not lie. But is that enough? There are other ways of misleading people than by lying. Geach tells the story of St. Athanasius, who "was rowing on a river when the persecutors

came rowing in the opposite direction: 'Where is the traitor Athanasius?' 'Not far away,' the Saint gaily replied, and rowed past them unsuspected."

Geach approves of Athanasius's deception even though he thinks it would have been wrong to tell an outright lie. Lying, Geach thinks, is always forbidden: a person possessing the virtue of honesty will not even consider it. Indeed, on his view that is what the virtues are: they are dispositions of character that simply *rule out* actions that are incompatible with them. Honest people will not lie, and so they will have to find other ways to deal with difficult situations. Athanasius was clever enough to do so. He told the truth, even if it was a deceptive truth.

Of course, it is hard to see why Athanasius's deception was not also dishonest. What nonarbitrary principle would approve of misleading people by one means but not by another? But whatever we think about this, the larger question is whether virtue requires adherence to absolute rules. Concerning honesty, we may distinguish two views of the matter:

1. That an honest person will never lie

and

2. That an honest person will never lie except in rare circumstances when there are compelling reasons why it must be done.

There is no obvious reason why the first view must be accepted. On the contrary, there is reason to favor the second. To see why, we need only to consider why lying is a bad thing in the first place. The explanation might go like this:

Our ability to live together in communities depends on our capacities of communication. We talk to one another, read one another's writing, exchange information and opinions, express our desires to one another, make promises, ask and answer questions, and much more. Without these sorts of interchanges, social living would be impossible. But in order for these interchanges to be successful, we must be able to assume that there are certain rules in force: we must be able to rely on one another to speak honestly.

Moreover, when we accept someone's word we make ourselves vulnerable to harm in a special way. By accepting what they say and modifying our beliefs accordingly, we place our welfare in their hands. If they speak truthfully, all is well. But if they lie, we end up with false beliefs; and if we act on those beliefs, we end up doing foolish things. It is *their fault:* we trusted them, and they let us down. This explains why being given the lie is distinctively offensive. It is at bottom a violation of trust. (It also explains, incidentally, why lies and "deceptive truths" may seem morally indistinguishable. Both may violate trust in the same fashion.)

None of this, however, implies that honesty is the *only* important value or that we have an obligation to deal honestly with *everyone* who comes along, regardless of who they are and what they are up to. Self-preservation is also an important matter, especially protecting ourselves from those who would harm us unjustly. When this comes into conflict with the rule against lying it is not unreasonable to think it takes priority. Suppose St. Athanasius had told the persecutors "I don't know him," and as a result they went off on a wild goose chase. Later, could they sensibly complain that he had violated their trust? Wouldn't they have forfeited any right they might have had to the truth from him when they set out unjustly to persecute him?

4. *Loyalty to Family and Friends.* At the beginning of Plato's dialogue *Euthyphro* Socrates learns that Euthyphro, whom he has encountered near the entrance to the court, has come there to prosecute his father for murder. Socrates expresses surprise at this and wonders whether it is proper for a son to bring charges against his father. Euthyphro sees no impropriety, however: for him, a murder is a murder. Unfortunately, the question is left unresolved as their discussion moves on to other matters.

The idea that there is something morally special about family and friends is, of course, familiar. We do not treat our family and friends as we would treat strangers. We are bound to them by love and affection and we do things for them that we would not do for just anybody. But this is not merely a matter of our being nicer to people we like. The nature of our relationships with family and friends is different from our relationships with other people, and part of the difference is that our *duties and responsibilities* are different. This seems to be an integral part of what friendship is. How could I be your friend and yet have no duty to treat you with special consideration?

If we needed proof that humans are essentially social creatures, the existence of friendship would supply all we could want. As Aristotle said, "No one would choose to live without friends, even if he had all other goods":

> How could prosperity be safeguarded and preserved without friends? The greater it is the greater are the risks it brings with it. Also, in poverty and all other kinds of misfortune men believe that their only refuge consists in their friends. Friends help young men avoid error; to older people they give the care and help needed to supplement the failing powers of action which infirmity brings.

Friends give help, to be sure, but the benefits of friendship go far beyond material assistance. Psychologically, we would be lost without friends. Our triumphs seem hollow unless we have friends to share them with, and our failures are made bearable by their understanding. Even our self-esteem depends in large measure on the assurances of friends: by returning our affection, they confirm our worthiness as human beings.

If we need friends, we need no less the qualities of character that enable us to *be* a friend. Near the top of the list is loyalty. Friends can be counted on. They stick by one another even when the going is hard, and even when, objectively speaking, the friend might deserve to be abandoned. They make allowances for one another; they forgive offenses and they refrain from harsh judgments. There are limits, of course: sometimes a friend will be the only one who can tell us hard truths about ourselves. But criticism is acceptable from friends because we know that, even if they scold us privately, they will not embarrass us in front of others.

None of this is to say that we do not have duties to other people, even to strangers. But they are different duties, associated with different virtues. Generalized beneficence is a virtue, and it may demand a great deal, but it does not require for strangers the same level of concern that we have for friends. Justice is another such virtue; it requires impartial treatment for all. But because friends are loyal, the demands of justice apply less certainly between them.

That is why Socrates is surprised to learn that Euthyphro is prosecuting his father. The relationship that we have with members of our family may be even closer than that of friendship; and so, as much as we might admire his passion for justice, we still may be startled that Euthyphro could take the same attitude toward his father that he would take toward someone else who had committed the same crime. It seems inconsistent with the proper regard of a son. The point is still recognized by the law today. In the United States, as well as in some other countries, a wife cannot be compelled to testify in court against her husband, and vice versa.

Why Are the Virtues Important? We said that virtues are traits of character that are good for people to have. This only raises the further question of *why* the virtues are desirable. Why is it a good thing for a person to be courageous, generous, honest, or loyal? The answer, of course, may vary depending on the particular virtue in question. Thus:

- Courage is a good thing because life is full of dangers and without courage we would be unable to cope with them.
- Generosity is desirable because some people will inevitably be worse off than others and they will need help.
- Honesty is needed because without it relations between people would go wrong in myriad ways.
- Loyalty is essential to friendship—friends stick by one another, even when they are tempted to turn away.

Looking at this list suggests that each virtue is valuable for a different reason. However, Aristotle believed it is possible to give a more general answer to our question: he thought that the virtuous person will fare better in life. The point is not that the virtuous will be richer—that is obviously not so, or at least it is not always so. The point is that the virtues are needed to conduct our lives well.

To see what Aristotle is getting at, consider the kinds of creatures we are and the kinds of lives we lead. On the most general level, we are rational and social beings who both want and need the company of other people. So we live in communities among friends, family, and fellow citizens. In this setting, such qualities as loyalty, fairness, and honesty are needed for interacting with all those other people successfully. (Imagine the difficulties that would be experienced by someone who habitually manifested the opposite qualities in his or her social life.) On a more individual level, our separate lives might include working at a particular kind of job and having particular sorts of interests. Other virtues may be necessary for successfully doing that job or pursuing those interests—perseverance and industriousness might be important. Again, it is part of our common human condition that we must sometimes face danger or temptation; and so courage and self-control are needed. The upshot is that, despite their differences, the virtues all have the same general sort of value: they are all qualities needed for successful human living.

Are the Virtues the Same for Everyone? Finally, we may ask whether there is *one* set of traits that is desirable for all people. Should we even speak of *the* good person, as though all good people come from a single mold? This assumption has often been challenged. Friedrich Nietzsche, for example, did not think that there is only one kind of human goodness. In his flamboyant way, Nietzsche observes:

> How naive it is altogether to say: "Man *ought* to be such-and-such!" Reality shows us an enchanting wealth of types, the abundance of a lavish play and change of forms—and some wretched loafer of a moralist comments: "No! Man ought to be different." He even knows what man should be like, this wretched bigot and prig: he paints himself on the wall and exclaims, *"Ecce homo!"*

There is obviously something to this. The scholar who devotes his life to understanding medieval literature and the professional soldier are very different kinds of people. A Victorian woman who would never expose a knee in public and a modern woman on a bathing-beach have very different standards of modesty. And yet all may be admirable in their own ways.

There is, then, an obvious sense in which the virtues may be thought of as differing from person to person. Because people lead different kinds of lives, have different sorts of personalities, and occupy different social roles, the qualities of character that they manifest may differ.

It is tempting to go even further and say simply that the virtues differ in different societies. After all, the kind of life that is possible for an individual will depend on the society in which he or she lives. A scholar's life is possible only in a society that has institutions, such as universities, that define and make possible the life of a scholar. The same could be said of a football player, a priest, or an interior decorator. Societies provide systems of values, institutions, and ways of life within which individual lives are fashioned. The traits of character that are needed to occupy these roles will differ, and so the traits needed to live successfully will differ. Thus the virtues will be different. In light of all this, why shouldn't we just say that which qualities are virtues will depend on the ways of life that are created and sustained by particular societies?

To this it may be countered that *there are some virtues that will be needed by all people in all times.* This was Aristotle's view, and he was probably right. Aristotle believed that we all have a great deal in common, despite our differences. "One may observe," he said, "in one's travels to distant countries the feelings of recognition and affiliation that link every human being to every other human being." Even in the most disparate societies, people face the same basic problems and have the same basic needs. Thus:

- Everyone needs courage, because no one (not even the scholar) is so safe that danger may not sometimes arise.
- In every society there will be property to be managed, and decisions to be made about who gets what, and in every society there will be some people who are worse off than others; so generosity is always to be prized.

- Honesty in speech is always a virtue because no society can exist without communication among its members.
- Everyone needs friends, and to have friends one must be a friend; so everyone needs loyalty.

This sort of list could—and in Aristotle's hands it does—go on and on.

To summarize, then, it may be true that in different societies the virtues are given somewhat different interpretations, and different sorts of actions are counted as satisfying them; and it may be true that some people, because they lead particular sorts of lives in particular sorts of circumstances, will have occasion to need some virtues more than others. But it cannot be right to say simply that whether any particular character trait is a virtue is never anything more than a matter of social convention. The major virtues are mandated not by social convention but by basic facts about our common human condition.

12.4. Some Advantages of Virtue Ethics

As we noted above, some philosophers believe that an emphasis on the virtues is superior to other ways of thinking about ethics. Why? A number of reasons have been suggested. Here are three of them.

1. *Moral motivation.* First, virtue ethics is appealing because it provides a natural and attractive account of moral motivation. The other theories seem deficient on this score. Consider the following example.

You are in the hospital recovering from a long illness. You are bored and restless, and so you are delighted when Smith arrives to visit. You have a good time chatting with him; his visit is just the tonic you needed. After a while you tell Smith how much you appreciate his coming: he really is a fine fellow and a good friend to take the trouble to come all the way across town to see you. But Smith demurs; he protests that he is merely doing his duty. At first you think Smith is only being modest, but the more you talk, the clearer it becomes that he is speaking the literal truth. He is not visiting you because he wants to, or because he likes you, but only because he thinks it is his duty to "do the right thing," and on this occasion he has decided it is his duty to visit you—perhaps because he knows of no one else who is more in need of cheering up or no one easier to get to.

This example was suggested by Michael Stocker in an influential article that appeared in the *Journal of Philosophy* in 1976. Stocker comments that surely you would be very disappointed to learn Smith's motive; now his visit seems cold and calculating and it loses all value to you. You thought he was your friend, but now you learn otherwise. Stocker says about Smith's behavior: "Surely there is something lacking here—and lacking in moral merit or value."

Of course, there is nothing wrong with what Smith *did*. The problem is his *motive*. We value friendship, love, and respect; and we want our relationships with people to be based on mutual regard. Acting from an abstract sense of duty, or from a desire to "do the right thing," is not the same. We would not want to live in a community of people who acted only from such motives, nor would we want to *be* such a person. Therefore, the argument goes, theories of ethics that emphasize only right action will never provide a completely satisfactory account of the moral life. For that, we need a theory that emphasizes personal qualities such as friendship, love, and loyalty—in other words, a theory of the virtues.

2. *Doubts about the "ideal" of impartiality.* A dominant theme of modern moral philosophy has been impartiality—the idea that all persons are morally equal, and that in deciding what to do we should treat everyone's interests as equally important. (Of the four theories of "right action" listed above, only Ethical Egoism, a theory with few adherents, denies this.) John Stuart Mill put the point well when he wrote that "Utilitarianism requires [the moral agent] to be as strictly impartial as a benevolent and disinterested spectator." The book you are now reading also treats impartiality as a fundamental moral requirement: in the first chapter impartiality was included as a part of the "minimum conception" of morality.

It may be doubted, though, whether impartiality is really such an important feature of the moral life. Consider one's relationships with family and friends. Are we really impartial where their interests are concerned? And should we be? A mother loves her children and cares for them in a way that she does not care for other children. She is partial to them through and through. But is there anything wrong with that? Isn't it exactly the way a mother *should* be? Again, we love our friends and we are willing to do things for them that we would not do for just anyone. Is there anything wrong with *that*? On the contrary, it seems that the love of family and friends is an inescapable feature of the morally good life. Any theory that emphasizes impartiality will have a difficult time accounting for this.

A moral theory that emphasizes the virtues, however, can account for all this very comfortably. Some virtues are partial and some are not. Love and friendship involve partiality toward loved ones and friends; beneficence toward people in general is also a virtue, but it is a virtue of a different kind. What is needed, on this view, is not some general requirement of impartiality, but an understanding of the nature of these different virtues and how they relate to one another.

3. *Virtue ethics and feminism.* Finally, we may notice a connection between the ethics of virtue and some concerns voiced by feminist thinkers. Feminists have argued that modern moral philosophy incorporates a subtle male bias. It isn't just that the most renowned philosophers have all been men, or that many of them have been guilty of sexist prejudice in what they have said about women. The bias is more systematic, deeper, and more interesting than that.

To see the bias, we need first to notice that social life has traditionally been divided into public and private realms, with men in charge of public affairs and women assigned responsibility for life's more personal and private dimensions. Men have dominated political and economic life, while women have been consigned to home and hearth. *Why* there has been this division would, in a different context, be a matter of some interest. Perhaps it is due to some inherent difference between men and women that suits them for the different roles. Or it may be merely a matter of social custom. But for present purposes, the cause of this arrangement need not concern us. It is enough to note that it has existed for a long time.

The public and private realms each have their own distinctive concerns. In politics and business, one's relations with other people are frequently impersonal and contractual. Often the relationship is adversarial—they have interests that conflict with our own. So we negotiate; we bargain and make deals. Moreover, in public life our decisions may affect large numbers of people whom we do not even know. So we may try to calculate, in an impersonal way, which decisions will have the best overall outcome for the most people.

In the world of home and hearth, however, things are different. It is a smaller-scale environment. In it, we are dealing mainly with family and friends, with whom our relationships are more personal and intimate. Bargaining and calculating play a much smaller role. Relations of love and caring are paramount.

Now with this in mind, think again about the theories of "right action" that have dominated modern moral philosophy—theories produced by male philosophers whose sensibilities were shaped by their own distinctive sorts of experience. The influence of that experience is plain. Their theories emphasize impersonal duty, contracts, the harmonization of competing interests, and the calculation of costs and benefits. The concerns that accompany private life—the realm in which women traditionally dominate—are almost wholly absent. The theory of virtue may be seen as a corrective to this imbalance. It can make a place for the virtues of private life as well as the rather different virtues that are required by public life. It is no accident that feminist philosophers are among those who are now most actively promoting the idea of a return to the ethics of virtue.

12.5. The Incompleteness of Virtue Ethics

The preceding arguments make an impressive case for two general points: first, that an adequate philosophical theory of ethics must provide an understanding of moral character; and second, that modern moral philosophers have failed to do this. Not only have they neglected the topic; what is more, their neglect has led them sometimes to embrace doctrines that *distort* the nature of moral character. Suppose we accept these conclusions. Where do we go from here?

One way of proceeding would be to develop a theory that combines the best features of the right action approach with insights drawn from the virtues approach—we might try to improve utilitarianism, Kantianism, and the like by adding to them a better account of moral character. Our total theory would then include an account of the virtues, but that account would be offered only as a supplement to a theory of right action. This sounds sensible, and if such a project could be carried out successfully, there would obviously be much to be said in its favor.

Some virtue theorists, however, have suggested that we should proceed differently. They have argued that the ethics of virtue should be considered as an *alternative* to the other sorts of theories—as an independent theory of ethics that is complete in itself. We might call this "radical virtue ethics." Is this a viable view?

Virtue and Conduct. As we have seen, theories that emphasize right action seem incomplete because they neglect the question of character. Virtue theory remedies this problem by making the question of character its central concern. But as a result, virtue theory runs the risk of being incomplete in the opposite way. Moral problems are frequently problems about what we should *do*. It is not obvious how, according to virtue theory, we should we go about deciding what to do. What can this approach tell us about the assessment, not of character, but of action?

The answer will depend on the spirit in which virtue theory is offered. If a theory of the virtues is offered only as a supplement to a theory of right action, then when the assessment of action is at issue the resources of the total theory will be brought into play and some version of utilitarian or Kantian policies (for example) will be recommended. On the other hand, if the theory of virtue is offered as an independent theory intended to be complete in itself, more drastic steps must be taken. Either the theory will have to jettison the notion of "right action" altogether or it will have to give some account of the notion derived from the conception of virtuous character.

Although it sounds at first like a crazy idea, some philosophers have in fact argued that we should simply get rid of such concepts as "morally right action." Anscombe says that "it would be a great improvement" if we stopped using such notions altogether. We could still assess conduct as better or worse, she says, but we would do so in other terms. Instead of saying that an action was "morally wrong" we would simply say that it was "untruthful" or "unjust"—terms derived from the vocabulary of virtue. On her view, we need not say anything more than this to explain why an action is to be rejected.

But it is not really necessary for radical virtue theorists to jettison such notions as "morally right." Such notions can be retained but given a new interpretation within the virtue framework. This might be done as follows. First, it could be said that actions are to be assessed as right or wrong in the familiar way, by reference to the reasons that can be given for or against them: we ought to do those actions that have the best reasons in their favor. However, *the reasons cited will all be reasons that are connected with the virtues*—the reasons in favor of doing an act will be that it is honest, or generous, or fair, and the like; while the reasons against doing it will be that it is dishonest, or stingy, or unfair, and the like. This analysis could be summed up by saying that our duty is to act virtuously—the "right thing to do," in other words, is whatever a virtuous person would do.

The Problem of Incompleteness. We have now sketched the radical virtue theorist's way of understanding what we ought to do. Is that understanding sufficient? The principal problem for the theory is the problem of incompleteness.

First, consider what it would mean in the case of a typical virtue—the virtue of honesty. Suppose a person is tempted to lie, perhaps because lying offers some advantage in a particular situation. The reason he or she should not lie, according to the radical virtue ethics approach, is simply because doing so would be dishonest. This sounds reasonable enough. But what does it mean to be honest? Isn't an honest person simply one who follows such rules as "Do not lie"? It is hard to see what honesty consists in if it is not the disposition to follow such rules.

But we cannot avoid asking *why* such rules are important.

Why shouldn't a person lie, especially when there is some advantage to be gained from it? Plainly we need an answer that goes beyond the simple observation that doing so would be incompatible with having a particular character trait; we need an explanation of why it is better to have this trait than its opposite. Possible answers might be that a policy of truth-telling is on the whole to one's own advantage; or that it promotes the general welfare; or that it is needed by people who must live together relying on one another. The first explanation looks suspiciously like Ethical Egoism; the second is utilitarian; and the third recalls contractarian ways of thinking. In any case, giving any explanation at all seems to take us beyond the limits of unsupplemented virtue theory.

Second, it is difficult to see how unsupplemented virtue theory could handle cases of moral *conflict*. Suppose you must choose between A and B, when it would be dishonest but kind to do A, and honest but unkind to do B. (An example might be telling the truth in circumstances that would be hurtful to someone.) Honesty and kindness are both virtues, and so there are reasons both for and against each alternative. But you must do one or the other—you must either tell the truth, and be unkind, or not tell the truth, and be dishonest. So which should you do? The admonition to act virtuously does not, by itself, offer much help. It only leaves you wondering which virtue takes precedence. It seems that we need some more general guidance, beyond that which radical virtue theory can offer, to resolve such conflicts.

Is There a Virtue That Matches Every Morally Good Reason for Doing Something? The problem of incompleteness points toward a more general theoretical difficulty for the radical virtue ethics approach. As we have seen, according to this approach the reasons for or against doing an action must always be associated with one or more virtues. Thus radical virtue ethics is committed to the idea that *for any good reason that may be given in favor of doing an action, there is a corresponding virtue that consists in the disposition to accept and act on that reason.* But this does not appear to be true.

Suppose, for example, that you are a legislator and you must decide how to allocate funds for medical research—

there isn't enough money for everything, and you must decide whether to invest resources in AIDS research or in some other worthy project. And suppose you decide it is best in these circumstances to do what will benefit the most people. Is there a virtue that matches the disposition to do this? If there is, perhaps it should be called "acting like a utilitarian." Or, to return to our example of moral conflicts—is there a virtue connected with every principle that can be invoked to resolve conflicts between the other virtues? If there is, perhaps it is the "virtue" of wisdom—which is to say, the ability to figure out and do what is on the whole best. But this gives away the game. If we posit such "virtues" only to make all moral decision making fit into the preferred framework, we will have saved radical virtue ethics, but at the cost of abandoning its central idea.

Conclusion. For these reasons, it seems best to regard the theory of virtue as part of an overall theory of ethics rather than as a complete theory in itself. The total theory would include an account of all the considerations that figure in practical decision making, together with their underlying rationale. The question, then, will be whether such a total view can accommodate *both* an adequate conception of right action *and* a related conception of virtuous character in a way that does justice to both.

I can see no reason why this is not possible. Our overall theory might begin by taking human welfare—or the welfare of all sentient creatures, for that matter—as the surpassingly important value. We might say that, from a moral point of view, we should want a society in which all people can lead happy and satisfying lives. We could then go on to consider both the question of what sorts of actions and social policies would contribute to this goal *and* the question of what qualities of character are needed to create and sustain individual lives. An inquiry into the nature of virtue could profitably be conducted from within the perspective that such a larger view would provide. Each could illuminate the other; and if each part of the overall theory has to be adjusted a bit here and there to accommodate the other, so much the better for truth.

CHAPTER 13

What Would a Satisfactory Moral Theory Be Like?

> Some people believe that there cannot be progress in Ethics, since everything has already been said. . . . I believe the opposite. . . . Compared with the other sciences, Non-Religious Ethics is the youngest and least advanced.
>
> DEREK PARFIT, *REASONS AND PERSONS* (1984)

13.1. Morality Without Hubris

Moral philosophy has a rich and fascinating history. A great many thinkers have approached the subject from a wide variety of perspectives and have produced theories that both attract and repel the thoughtful reader. Almost all the classical theories contain plausible elements, which is hardly surprising, considering that they were devised by philosophers of undoubted genius. Yet the various theories are not consistent with one another, and most are vulnerable to crippling objections. After reviewing them, one is left wondering what to believe. What, in the final analysis, is the truth? Of course, different philosophers would answer this question in different ways. Some might refuse to answer at all, on the grounds that we do not yet know enough to have reached the "final analysis." (In this, moral philosophy is not much worse off than any other subject of human inquiry—we do not know the final truth about almost anything.) But we do know a lot, and it may not be unduly rash to venture a guess as to what a satisfactory moral theory might be like.

A satisfactory theory would, first of all, be sensitive to the facts about human nature, and it would be appropriately modest about the place of human beings in the scheme of things. The universe is some 16 billion years old—that is the time elapsed since the "big bang"—and the earth itself was formed about 4.6 billion years ago. The evolution of life on the planet was a slow process, guided not by design but (largely) by random mutation and natural selection. The first humans appeared quite recently. The extinction of the great dinosaurs 65 million years ago (possibly as the result of a catastrophic collision between the earth and an asteroid) left ecological room for the evolution of the few little mammals that were about, and after 63 or 64 million *more* years, one line of that evolution finally produced us. In geological time, we arrived only yesterday.

But no sooner did our ancestors arrive than they began to think of themselves as the most important things in all creation. Some of them even imagined that the whole universe had been made for their benefit. Thus, when they began to develop theories of right and wrong, they held that the protection of their own interests had a kind of ultimate and objective value. The rest of creation, they reasoned, was intended for their use. We now know better. We now know that we exist by evolutionary accident, as one species among many, on a small and insignificant world in one little corner of the cosmos.

Hume, who knew only a little of this story, nevertheless realized that human *hubris* is largely unjustified. "The life of a man," he wrote, "is of no greater importance to the universe than that of an oyster." But he also recognized that our lives are important to *us*. We are creatures with desires, needs, plans, and hopes; and even if "the universe" does not care about those things, we do. Our theory of morality may begin from this point. In order to have a convenient name for it, let us call this theory *Morality Without Hubris*—or *MWH* for short. MWH incorporates some elements of the various classical theories while rejecting others.

Human *hubris* is largely unjustified, but it is not *entirely* unjustified. Compared to the other creatures on earth, we do have impressive intellectual capacities. We have evolved as rational beings. This fact gives some point to our inflated opinion of ourselves; and, as it turns out, it is also what makes us capable of having a morality. Because we are rational, we are able to take some facts as *reasons* for behaving one way rather than another. We can articulate those reasons and think about them. Thus we take the fact that an action would help satisfy our desires, needs, and so on—in short, the fact that an action would *promote our interests*—as a reason in favor of doing that action. And of course we take the fact that an action would frustrate our interests as a reason against doing it.

The origin of our concept of "ought" may be found in these facts. If we were not capable of considering reasons for and against actions, we would have no use for such a notion. Like the lower animals, we would simply act from impulse or habit, or as Kant put it, from "inclination." But the consideration of reasons introduces a new factor. Now we find ourselves impelled to act in certain ways as a result of deliberation, as a result of thinking about our behavior and its consequences. We use the word "ought" to mark this new element of the situation: we *ought* to do the act supported by the weightiest reasons.

Once we consider morality as a matter of acting on reason, another important point emerges. In reasoning about what to do, we can be consistent or inconsistent. One way of being inconsistent is to accept a fact as a reason for action on one occasion, while refusing to accept a similar fact as a reason on another occasion, even though there is no difference between the two occasions that would justify distinguishing them. (This is the legitimate point made by Kant's Categorical Imperative. At the end of Chapter 9, I referred to this as his "basic idea.") This happens, for example, when a person unjustifiably places the interests of his own race or social group above the comparable interests of other races and social groups. Racism means counting the interest of the members of other races as less important than the interests of the members of one's own race, despite the fact that there is no general difference between the races that would justify it. It is an offense against morality because it is first an offense against reason. Similar remarks could be made about other doctrines that divide humanity into the morally favored and disfavored, such as egoism, sexism, and (some forms of) nationalism. The upshot is that reason requires impartiality: we ought to act so as to promote the interests of everyone alike.

If Psychological Egoism were true, this would mean that reason demands more of us than we can manage. But Psychological Egoism is not true; it gives an altogether false picture of human nature and the human condition. We have evolved as social creatures, living together in groups, wanting one another's company, needing one another's cooperation, and capable of caring about one another's welfare. So there is a pleasing theoretical "fit" between (a) what reason requires, namely impartiality; (b) the requirements of social living, namely adherence to a set of rules that, if fairly applied, would serve everyone's interests; and (c) our natural inclination to care about others, at least to a modest degree. All three work together to make morality not only possible, but in an important sense natural, for us.

So far, MWH sounds very much like Utilitarianism. However, there is one other fact about human beings that must be taken into account, and doing so will give the theory a decidedly non-utilitarian twist. As rational agents, humans have the power of choice: they may choose to do what they see to be right, or they may choose to do wrong. Thus they are *responsible* for their freely chosen actions, and they are judged morally good if they choose well or wicked if they choose badly. This, I think, has two consequences. First, it helps to explain why freedom is among the most cherished human values. A person who is denied the right to choose his or her own actions is thereby denied the possibility of achieving any kind of personal moral worth. Second, the way a person may be treated by others depends, to some extent, on the way he or she has chosen to treat them. One who treats others well deserves to be treated well in return, while one who treats others badly deserves to be treated badly in return.

This last point is liable to sound a little strange, so let me elaborate it just a bit. Suppose Smith has always been generous to others, helping them whenever he could; now he is in trouble and needs help in return. There is now a *special* reason *he* should be helped, above the general obligation we have to promote the interests of everyone alike. He is not just another member of the crowd. He is a particular person who, by his own previous conduct, has *earned* our respect and gratitude. But now consider someone with the opposite history: suppose Jones is your neighbor, and he has always *refused* to help you when you needed it. One day your car wouldn't start, for example, and Jones wouldn't give you a lift to work—he had no particular excuse, he just wouldn't be bothered. Imagine that, after this episode, Jones has car trouble and he has the nerve to ask you for a ride. Perhaps you think you should help him anyway, despite his own lack of helpfulness. (You might think that this will teach him generosity.) Nevertheless, if we concentrate on what he *deserves,* we must conclude that he deserves to be left to fend for himself.

Adjusting our treatment of individuals to match how they themselves have chosen to treat others is not just a matter of rewarding friends and holding grudges against enemies. It is a matter of treating people as *responsible agents,* who by their own choices show themselves to be deserving of particular responses, and toward whom such emotions as gratitude and resentment are appropriate. There is an important difference between Smith and Jones; why shouldn't that be reflected in the way we respond to them? What would it be like if we did *not* tailor our responses to people in this way? For one thing, we would be denying people (including ourselves) the ability to earn good treatment at the hands of others. Morally speaking, we would all become simply members of the great crowd of humanity, rather than individuals with particular personalities and deserts. Respecting people's right to choose their own conduct, and then adjusting our treatment of them according to how they choose, is ultimately a matter of "respect for persons" in a sense somewhat like Kant's.

We are now in a position to summarize the outline of what, in my judgment, a satisfactory moral theory would be like. Such a theory would see morality as based on facts about our nature and interests, rather than on some exaggerated conception of our "importance." As for the principles on which we ought to act, the theory is a combination of two ideas: first, that *we ought to act so as to promote the interests of everyone alike;* and second, that *we should treat people as they deserve to be treated, considering how they have themselves chosen to behave.*

But now the key question is: How are these two ideas related? How do they fit together to form a unified principle of conduct? They are not to be understood as entirely independent of one another. The first establishes a general presumption in favor of promoting everyone's interests, impartially; and the second specifies grounds on which this presumption may be overridden. Thus the second thought functions as a qualification to the first; it specifies that we may sometimes *depart from* a policy of "equal treatment" on the grounds that a person has shown by his past behavior that he deserves some particular response. We may therefore combine them into a single principle. The primary rule of morality, according to MWH, is:

> *We ought to act so as to promote impartially the interests of everyone alike, except when individuals deserve particular responses as a result of their own past behavior.*

This principle combines the best elements of both Utilitarianism and Kantian "respect for persons," but it is not produced simply by stitching those two philosophies together. Rather, it springs naturally from a consideration of the main facts of the human condition—that we are perishable beings with interests that may be promoted or frustrated, and that we are rational beings responsible for our conduct. Although more needs to be said about the theoretical basis of this view, I will say no more about it here. Instead I will turn to some of its practical implications. Like every moral theory, MWH implies that we should behave in certain ways; and in some cases, it implies that commonly accepted patterns of behavior are wrong and should be changed. The plausibility of the theory will depend in part on how successful it is in convincing us that our behavior should conform to its directives.

13.2. The Moral Community

When we are deciding what to do, whose interests should we take into account? People have answered this question in different ways at different times: egoists have said that one's own interests are all-important; racists have restricted moral concern to their own race; and nationalists have held that moral concern stops at the borders of one's country. The answer given by MWH is that *we ought to give equal consideration to the interests of everyone who will be affected by our conduct.* In principle, the community with which we should be concerned is limited only by the number of individuals who have interests, and that, as we shall see, is a very large number indeed.

This may seem a pious platitude, but in reality it can be a hard doctrine. As this is being written, for example, there is famine in Ethiopia and millions of people are starving. People in the affluent countries have not responded very well. There has been some aid given, but relatively few people have felt personally obligated to help by sending contributions to famine-relief agencies. People would no doubt feel a greater sense of obligation if it were their neighbors starving, rather than strangers in a foreign country. But on the theory we are considering, the location of the starving people makes no difference: *everyone* is included in the community of moral concern. This has radical consequences: for example, when a person is faced with the choice between spending ten dollars on a trip to the movies or contributing it for famine relief, he should ask himself which action would most effectively promote human welfare, with each person's interests counted as equally important. Would he benefit more from seeing the movie than a starving person would from getting food? Clearly, he would not. So he should contribute the money for famine relief. If this sort of reasoning were taken seriously, it would make an enormous difference in our responses to such emergencies.

If the moral community is not limited to people in one place, neither is it limited to people at any one *time.* Whether people will be affected by our actions now or in the distant future makes no difference. Our obligation is to consider all their interests equally. This is an important point because, with the development of nuclear weapons, we now have the capacity to alter the course of history in an especially dramatic way. Some argue that a full-scale nuclear war would result in the extinction of the human race. The prediction of "nuclear winter" supports this conclusion. The idea is that the detonation of so many nuclear devices would send millions of tons of dust and ash into the stratosphere, where it would block the sun's rays. The surface of the earth would become cold. This condition would persist for years, and the ecology would collapse. Those who were "lucky" enough to escape death earlier would perish in the nuclear winter. Other theorists contend that this estimate is too pessimistic. Civilization might come to an end, they say, and most people might die, but a few would survive and the long upward struggle would begin again.

Considering this, it is difficult to imagine any circumstances in which the large-scale use of nuclear weapons would be justified. With the transformation of the Soviet Union, of course, we now have reason to think that nuclear war is less likely, especially in the immediate future. But the longer-range future remains uncertain. The weapons still exist, and with each passing decade more nations have them; so the worry about their use is not likely to go away. What makes their use morally problematic is not just that, in using them, we would likely destroy ourselves. In the larger historical context, our interests are of only passing importance. The evil of condemning future generations to the miseries of a post-nuclear war age would also be a part of our moral record.

There is one other way in which our conception of the moral community must be expanded. Humans, as we have noted, are only one species of animal inhabiting this planet. Like humans, the other animals also have interests that are affected by what we do. When we kill or torture them, they are harmed, just as humans are harmed when treated in those ways. The utilitarians were right to insist that the interests of nonhuman animals must be given weight in our moral calculations. As Bentham pointed out, excluding creatures from moral consideration because of their species is no more justified than excluding them because of race, nationality, or sex. I have already discussed the relevant arguments on this point (in Chapter 7), so I will not repeat that discussion here. Here I will only point out again that impartiality requires the expansion of the moral community—not only across space and time but across the boundaries of species as well.

13.3. Justice and Fairness

MWH has much in common with Utilitarianism, especially in what I called MWH's "first idea." But as we saw in Chapter 8, Utilitarianism has been severely criticized for failing to account for the values of justice and fairness. Can MWH do any better in this regard? It does, because it makes a person's past behavior relevant to how he or she should be treated. This introduces into the theory an acknowledgment of personal merit that is lacking in unqualified Utilitarianism.

One specific criticism of Utilitarianism had to do with its implications for the institution of punishment. We can imagine cases in which it promotes the general welfare to frame an innocent person, which is blatantly unjust; and taking the Principle of Utility as our ultimate standard, it is hard to explain why this is so. More generally, as Kant pointed out, the basic utilitarian "justification" of punishment is in terms of treating individuals as mere "means." MWH provides a different view of the matter. In punishing someone, we are treating him differently from the way we treat others—punishment involves a failure of impartiality. But this is justified, on our account, by the person's own past deeds. It is a response to what he has done. That is why it is not right to frame an innocent person; the innocent person has not done anything to deserve being singled out for such treatment. The account of punishment suggested by MWH is very close to Kant's.

The theory of punishment, however, is only one small part of the subject of justice. Questions of justice arise any time one person is treated differently from another. Suppose an employer must choose which of two employees to promote, when he can promote only one of them. The first candidate has worked hard for the company, taking on extra work when it was needed, giving up her vacation to help out, and so on. The second candidate, on the other hand, has always done only the minimum required of him. (And we will assume he has no excuse; he has simply *chosen* not to work very hard for the company.) Obviously, the two employees will be treated very differently: one will get the promotion; the other will not. But this is all right, according to our theory, because the first employee deserves to be advanced over the second, considering the past performance of each. The first employee has earned the promotion, the second has not.

This is an easy case, in that it is obvious what the employer should do. But it illustrates an important difference between our theory and Utilitarianism. Utilitarians might argue that their theory also yields the right decision in this case. They might observe that it promotes the general welfare for companies to reward hard work; therefore the Principle of Utility, unsupplemented by any further consideration, would also say that the first employee, but not the second, should be promoted. Perhaps this is so. Nevertheless, this is unsatisfactory because it has the first employee being promoted for the *wrong reason*. She has a claim on the promotion because of her own hard work, and not simply because promoting her would be better for us all. MWH accommodates this vital point, whereas Utilitarianism does not.

MWH holds that a person's voluntary actions can justify departures from the basic policy of "equal treatment," but *nothing else can*. This goes against a common view of the matter. Often, people think it is right for individuals to be rewarded for physical beauty, superior intelligence, or other native endowments. (In practice, people often get better jobs and a greater share of life's good things just because they were born with greater natural gifts.) But on reflection, this does not seem right. People do not deserve their native endowments; they have them as a result of what John Rawls has called "the natural lottery." Suppose the first employee in our example was passed over for the promotion, despite her hard work, because the second employee had some native talent that was more useful in the new position. Even if the employer could justify this decision in terms of the company's needs, the first employee would rightly feel that there is something unfair going on. She has worked harder, yet he is now getting the promotion, and the benefits that go with it, because of something he did nothing to merit. That is not fair. A just society, according to MWH, would be one in which people may improve their positions through work (with the opportunity for work available to everyone), but they would not enjoy superior positions simply because they were born lucky.

I cannot, here, provide a full defense of this controversial idea. However, I can make it somewhat more plausible by showing how it helps to resolve an important contemporary issue. Our theory points the way toward a solution to one of the most vexing problems of social justice now being debated—the problem of reverse discrimination.

The problem of reverse discrimination is complex, but we can capture its most important elements in a simple example. Two college seniors, one black and one white, apply for admission to a certain law school. Both have grades and test scores well above the minimum required for admission, but the white student's qualifications are slightly superior to the black's. Nevertheless, the black applicant is accepted while the white applicant is rejected. When the white student asks why, he is told that the competition is stiff, and that a certain number of places in each entering class are reserved for minority applicants. This is part of the school's response to the fact that in the past, blacks have been denied the same opportunities as whites. As a result of this discrimination, blacks are under-represented in the legal profession; and the school's policy of preferential admission is an attempt to help remedy this undesirable situation.

In the 1970s, many schools in the United States had such policies. They came under sharp attack. Today there are fewer. The critics complained that such policies were no better than the old discredited forms of discrimination. Considering my example, they would say that the white student is being rejected simply because he is white (if he had been black, with the same qualifications, he would have been accepted), and this is just as objectionable as rejecting black applicants because they are black. Moreover, they would say, it is unfair to the white student: *he* is not responsible for the harm that has been done to blacks, so why should he now be penalized in the effort to make up for it? In 1978, in the case of *California* v. *Bakke*, the U.S. Supreme Court sided with the critics and ruled that preferential "quotas" were unconstitutional.

Often, critics have suggested that we distinguish policies of reverse discrimination from less drastic policies of "preferential treatment" or "affirmative action." The latter do not go as far as the law school policy in our example. They merely require that positive steps be taken to ensure that minority candidates receive equal consideration for jobs, school admissions, and so forth. At most, these less radical policies might involve preferring blacks in competitive situations in which they are *equally* qualified. But in our example, the black student is admitted ahead of the white even though he is *less* qualified. Thus the example poses the problem in its strongest form. I have deliberately chosen to frame the example in this way because if it could be shown that there is no moral objection to the law school's action in this case, we would have the strongest possible defense of such policies.

Is the law school's action defensible? The question provokes strong emotions, and it is difficult for most people to consider it dispassionately. I believe, however, that if we do think dispassionately, we will find that the answer depends on *why* the white student's grades, test scores, etc., are better than the black's. The key question is: *What accounts for* the fact that the white student is better qualified?

Suppose, first, that the explanation is simply that the white student has worked harder to achieve his present status. He has studied diligently; he has deliberately taken more difficult courses; and when he has had to choose between studying and partying, he has generally chosen to study. Meanwhile the black student, who has had the same opportunities, has chosen a different course. He has not worked very hard; he has avoided the difficult subjects in school; he has spent a lot of time enjoying himself; and so on. As a result of this, the white student can now present a better record for the law school's consideration. If *this* is what accounts for the difference in their qualifications, then the white applicant really has been treated unfairly. He has earned his superior qualifications; he deserves to be admitted ahead of the black student because he has worked harder for it.

But now suppose a different explanation is given as to why the white student has ended up with superior qualifications. Suppose the applicants have worked equally hard. However, the white student has had a much easier time of it because he has had gifted teachers, the most up-to-date facilities, and so on, while the black student, by contrast, has had to contend with many obstacles. For example, his early education may have been at the hands of ill-trained teachers in crowded, inadequate schools, so that by the time he reached college he was far behind the other students, and despite his best efforts he never could quite catch up. If *this* is what accounts for the difference in qualifications, things look very different. For now the white student has not *earned* his superior qualifications. *He* has done nothing to deserve them. The difference in qualifications is due entirely to the white student's good luck in having been born into a more advantaged social position. Surely he cannot deserve to be admitted into law school ahead of the black simply because of *that.*

In fact, black people in the United States have been, and are, systematically discriminated against, and it is reasonable to believe that this mistreatment does make a difference in their ability to compete for such goods as law school admission. Therefore, at least some actual cases probably do correspond to the second explanation. Some whites are better able to compete because they do not have to contend with the obstacles that have been placed in the way of blacks. If so, their ability to compete more successfully is not a sign that they are more deserving. This is a clear application of the idea mentioned above that the natural advantages of birth are not legitimate bases of desert.

It follows that in such a case the rejected white student is not being treated unfairly. He is not being rejected simply because he is white. The effect of the policy in question is only to *neutralize an advantage* that he has had because he is white, and that is very different. Nor will it do any good for the white to complain that, although blacks may have suffered unjust hardships, *he* is not responsible for it and so should not be penalized for it. The white student is not being "penalized" at all. Rather, he is not being allowed to *profit* from the fact that those wrongs were done, by besting the black in a competition that seems "fair" only if we ignore the handicaps imposed on only one competitor. This argument seems persuasive to me, and because it fits perfectly with the theory we have developed, it increases my confidence in that theory.

As I said at the outset, MWH represents my best guess about what an ultimately satisfactory moral theory might be like. I say "guess" not to indicate any lack of confidence; in my opinion, MWH *is* a satisfactory moral theory. However, it is instructive to remember that a great many thinkers have tried to devise such a theory, and history has judged them to have been only partially successful. This suggests that it would be wise not to make too grandiose a claim for one's own view. Moreover, as the Oxford philosopher Derek Parfit has observed, the earth will remain habitable for another billion years, and civilization is now only a few thousand years old. If we do not destroy ourselves, moral philosophy, along with all the other human inquiries, may yet have a long way to go.

Suggestions for Further Reading

General Suggestions

The book you are holding in your hands introduces moral philosophy by examining the most important general theories of ethics. There are other ways to approach the subject. Alasdair MacIntyre's *A Short History of Ethics* (New York: Macmillan, 1966) is an accessible historical treatment. Peter Singer's *Practical Ethics* (Cambridge: Cambridge University Press, 1979) is recommended as an introduction centered on such practical issues as abortion, racism, and so forth. *Matters of Life and Death,* edited by Tom Regan, 3rd ed. (New York: McGraw-Hill, 1993) is a good collection of introductory essays by various writers. The fact that these books are "introductions" should not be taken to mean that they are boringly elementary; each contains material that will be of interest even to sophisticated readers.

Chapter 1: What Is Morality?

The seventh chapter of *Classic Cases in Medical Ethics,* by Gregory E. Pence (New York: McGraw-Hill, 1990), is an especially good presentation of all the factual information about Baby Jane Doe; it also contains much useful background information, as well as a good philosophical discussion. *Should the Baby Live?,* by Peter Singer and Helga Kuhse (Oxford: Oxford University Press, 1985), is also recommended, as is an article by Nat Hentoff, "The Awful Privacy of Baby Doe," *Atlantic,* January 1985, pp. 54ff. (These two sources provide discussions from opposing points of view.)

    The Definition of Morality, edited by G. Wallace and A. D. M. Walker (London: Methuen, 1970), is a useful collection of articles by leading philosophers on the question of what morality is. For additional reflections on the place of reason in ethics, and its limitations, see J. Rachels, "Can Ethics Provide Answers?" in *Ethics in Hard Times,* edited by Arthur L. Caplan and Daniel Callahan (New York: Plenum, 1981). On the idea of impartiality, see Peter Singer, "Is Racism Arbitrary?" *Philosophia,* vol. 8 (1978), pp. 185–204. The same issue of *Philosophia* contains other helpful articles on racism.

Chapter 2: The Challenge of Cultural Relativism

Two classic defenses of Cultural Relativism by social scientists are Ruth Benedict, *Patterns of Culture* (New York: Pelican, 1946); and William Graham Sumner, *Folkways* (Boston: Ginn and Company, 1906). Kai Nielsen's essay "Ethical Relativism and the Facts of Cultural Relativity," *Social Research*, vol. 33 (1966), pp. 531–551, is an excellent philosophical discussion of the significance, or lack of it, of anthropological data.

Ethical Relativism, edited by John Ladd (Belmont, Calif.: Wadsworth, 1973), is a good collection of articles on Cultural Relativism. *Relativism: Cognitive and Moral*, edited by Jack W. Meiland and Michael Krausz (Notre Dame: University of Notre Dame Press, 1982), is another useful anthology.

Chapter 3: Subjectivism in Ethics

David Hume defended an important version of Ethical Subjectivism in Book III of his *A Treatise of Human Nature* (London, 1738; today available in numerous editions). But perhaps his clearest and most readable presentation of the theory is to be found in Section I and Appendix I of his *An Inquiry Concerning the Principles of Morals* (London, 1752; also available now in various editions).

In Chapter 3 of his little book *Ethics* (London: Oxford University Press, 1912), G. E. Moore gives the classic critique of Simple Subjectivism. C. L. Stevenson discusses Moore's arguments, and points out that they do not refute Emotivism, in "Moore's Arguments Against Certain Forms of Ethical Naturalism," which is included in the volume of Stevenson's collected essays *Facts and Values* (New Haven: Yale University Press, 1963). Reading Stevenson's essays is easier than attempting his great work *Ethics and Language* (New Haven: Yale University Press, 1944).

The literature on Emotivism is immense; one accessible critical work is J. O. Urmson, *The Emotive Theory of Ethics* (London: Hutchinson, 1968). Chapter 3 of G. J. Warnock's *Contemporary Moral Philosophy* (London: Macmillan, 1967) is also recommended.

Chapter 4: Does Morality Depend on Religion?

Two anthologies contain a wealth of material on this subject: *Religion and Morality*, edited by Gene Outka and John P. Reeder, Jr.

(Garden City, N.Y.: Anchor, 1973); and *Divine Commands and Morality,* edited by Paul Helm (Oxford: Oxford University Press, 1981). Both contain articles that defend the Divine Command Theory—such as Robert Merrihew Adams's "A Modified Divine Command Theory of Ethical Wrongness"—as well as critical papers. Norman Kretzmann's "Abraham, Isaac, and Euthyphro: God and the Basis of Morality," in *Hamartia,* edited by Donald Stump (Lewiston, N.Y.: Edw. Mellen Press, 1983) is a splendid essay, although it may be difficult to find. Kai Nielsen's *Ethics Without God* (London: Pemberton, 1973) is also recommended.

   Aquinas and Natural Law by D. J. O'Connor (London: Macmillan, 1968) is a good introductory treatment of the theory of natural law.

   The literature on abortion is, of course, vast. Some of the best philosophical articles are collected in *The Problem of Abortion,* edited by Joel Feinberg, 2nd ed. (Belmont, Calif.: Wadsworth, 1984). Perhaps the easiest way into the philosophical debate is through Chapter 6 of Peter Singer's *Practical Ethics* (Cambridge: Cambridge University Press, 1979). One of the most important, but also most difficult, philosophical studies of abortion is Michael Tooley, *Abortion and Infanticide* (Oxford: Clarendon Press, 1983). See, too, Barbara Baum Levenbook's and Joel Feinberg's essay "Abortion" in *Matters of Life and Death,* edited by Tom Regan, 3rd ed. (New York: McGraw-Hill, 1993).

Chapter 5: Psychological Egoism

Thomas Hobbes defends Psychological Egoism in certain passages in his *Leviathan* (London, 1651) and in *On Human Nature* (London, 1650). The former work is available today in various editions; the latter may be found in Thomas Hobbes, *Body, Man, and Citizen,* edited by Richard S. Peters (New York: Collier, 1962). Hobbes's view of human nature provoked much criticism; Joseph Butler's demolition of Psychological Egoism in his *Fifteen Sermons Preached at Rolls Chapel* (Oxford, 1726) is especially noteworthy.

   Among contemporary writings, Joel Feinberg's essay "Psychological Egoism," in *Reason and Responsibility,* edited by Feinberg (Encino, Calif.: Dickenson, 1965), stands out as a model of exposition and argument. Feinberg rejects the theory. A contemporary defense is Michael Slote, "An Empirical Basis for Psychological Egoism," *Journal of Philosophy,* vol. 61 (1964), pp. 530–537.

Chapter 6: Ethical Egoism

On our duty to contribute for famine relief, see William Aiken and Hugh LaFollette, eds., *World Hunger and Moral Obligation* (Englewood Cliffs, N.J.: Prentice-Hall, 1977); George R. Lucas, Jr., ed., *Lifeboat Ethics* (New York: Harper & Row, 1976); Peter G. Brown and Henry Shue, eds., *Food Policy* (New York: Free Press, 1977); and Onora O'Neill, "The Moral Perplexities of Famine Relief," in *Matters of Life and Death*, edited by Tom Regan, 2nd ed. (New York: Random House, 1985).

Alasdair MacIntyre, "Egoism and Altruism," in *The Encyclopedia of Philosophy*, edited by Paul Edwards (New York: Macmillan and Free Press, 1967), vol. 2, pp. 462–466, is a nice survey article. This 8-volume *Encyclopedia* is, by the way, a terrific reference work, with which everyone who is interested in philosophy ought to be familiar.

Robert G. Olson, *The Morality of Self-Interest* (New York: Harcourt, 1965), is the best contemporary work by a philosopher sympathetic to Ethical Egoism. The following articles amount to a more or less continuous debate about the merits of the theory: Brian Medlin, "Ultimate Principles and Ethical Egoism," *Australasian Journal of Philosophy*, vol. 35 (1957), pp. 111–118; John Hospers, "Baier and Medlin on Ethical Egoism," *Philosophical Studies*, vol. 12 (1961), pp. 10–16; W. H. Baumer, "Indefensible Impersonal Egoism," *Philosophical Studies*, vol. 18 (1967), pp. 72–75; Jesse Kalin, "On Ethical Egoism," *American Philosophical Quarterly Monograph Series, No. 1: Studies in Moral Philosophy* (1968), pp. 26–41; and James Rachels, "Two Arguments Against Ethical Egoism," *Philosophia*, vol. 4 (1974), pp. 297–314.

Chapter 7: The Utilitarian Approach

The indispensable classic work is John Stuart Mill's *Utilitarianism* (London, 1861). It is included in a collection, *Mill's Ethical Writings*, edited by J. B. Schneewind (New York: Collier, 1965), which also contains Mill's important essay on Bentham.

For more about euthanasia, see James Rachels, *The End of Life* (Oxford: Oxford University Press, 1986).

Peter Singer's *Animal Liberation* (New York: New York Review Books, 1975) is the book that made the question of animal welfare a topic of serious discussion among contemporary philosophers. It is lively, nontechnical, and easy to read. Also accessible is Singer's "Animals and the Value of Life" in *Matters of Life and Death,* edited by Tom Regan, 3rd ed. (New York: McGraw-Hill, 1993). See also various essays in *Animal Rights and Human Obligations,* edited by Tom Regan and Peter Singer, 2nd ed. (Englewood Cliffs, N.J.: Prentice-Hall, 1989), for a collection of readings representing diverse points of view. Tom Regan's *The Case for Animal Rights* (Berkeley: University of California Press, 1983) is the most recent and most thorough defense of animal rights; and R. G. Frey's *Rights, Killing, and Suffering: Moral Vegetarianism and Applied Ethics* (Oxford: Blackwell, 1983) is the best presentation of the case on the other side.

Chapter 8: The Debate over Utilitarianism

In two books, the English philosopher W. D. Ross presented an uncompromising attack on Utilitarianism: *The Right and the Good* (Oxford: Oxford University Press, 1930) and *Foundations of Ethics* (Oxford: Oxford University Press, 1939). After Ross, much of the contemporary debate was carried on in the academic journals. There is an *enormous* number of articles debating the merits of the theory. Two useful collections contain some of the most important ones: Samuel Gorovitz, ed., *Mill: Utilitarianism—Text and Critical Essays* (Indianapolis: Bobbs-Merrill, 1971); and Michael D. Bayles, ed., *Contemporary Utilitarianism* (Garden City, N.Y.: Anchor, 1968).

Also recommended are J. J. C. Smart and Bernard Williams, *Utilitarianism: For and Against* (Cambridge: Cambridge University Press, 1973); and Richard B. Brandt, *A Theory of the Good and the Right* (Oxford: Clarendon, 1979).

Chapter 9: Are There Absolute Moral Rules?

The best translations of Kant's major ethical writings are *Foundations of the Metaphysics of Morals,* translated by Lewis White Beck (Indianapolis: Bobbs-Merrill, 1959); *Critique of Practical Reason,* translated by Lewis White Beck (Indianapolis: Bobbs-Merrill, 1956); *The Metaphysical Principles of Virtue,* translated by James Ellington (Indianapolis: Bobbs-Merrill, 1964); *The Metaphysical Elements of Justice,* translated by John Ladd (Indianapolis: Bobbs-Merrill, 1965); and *Lectures on Ethics,* translated by Louis Infield (New York: Harper, 1963).

H. B. Acton's *Kant's Moral Philosophy* (London: Macmillan, 1970) is a good short work on Kant. Robert Paul Wolff, ed., *Kant: Foundations of the Metaphysics of Morals—Text and Critical Essays* (Indianapolis: Bobbs-Merrill, 1969), is a helpful collection of writings on Kant's ethics by a variety of philosophers.

A contemporary debate about absolute moral rules may be traced through the following articles: G. E. M. Anscombe, "Modern Moral Philosophy," *Philosophy,* vol. 33 (1958); Jonathan Bennett, " 'Whatever the Consequences,' " *Analysis,* vol. 26 (1966); P. T. Geach, *God and the Soul* (London: Routledge and Kegan Paul, 1969), Chapter 9; and James Rachels, "On Moral Absolutism," *Australasian Journal of Philosophy,* vol. 48 (1970).

Chapter 10: Kant and Respect for Persons

The best translations of Kant's writings are listed above. R. S. Downie and Elizabeth Telfer, *Respect for Persons* (London: Allen and Unwin, 1969), is a useful treatment of this concept. But perhaps the best introduction to the notion of Kantian respect is to be found in Herbert Morris's essay "Persons and Punishment," *The Monist,* vol. 52 (1968), pp. 475–501. Even though Morris does not specifically set out to explain Kant, his argument is so clear and so Kantian that understanding Morris's point is an excellent way of coming to understand what Kant had in mind.

The philosophical debate about the nature and justification of punishment is chronicled in two useful anthologies: *Philosophical Perspectives on Punishment,* edited by Gertrude Ezorsky (Albany: State University of New York Press, 1972); and *The Philosophy of Punishment,* edited by H. B. Acton (London: Macmillan, 1969). On capital punishment, see Hugo A. Bedau, *The Death Penalty in America* (Garden City, N.Y.: Anchor, 1964) and "Capital Punishment," in *Matters of Life and Death,* edited by Tom Regan, 3rd ed. (New York: McGraw-Hill, 1993). On the idea of "rehabilitation," see the splendid work prepared by the American Friends Service Committee, *Struggle for Justice* (New York: Hill and Wang, 1971).

Chapter 11: The Idea of a Social Contract

The classic works are Thomas Hobbes, *Leviathan* (1651); John Locke, *The Second Treatise of Government* (1690); and Jean Jacques Rousseau, *The Social Contract* (1762). All are available today in various editions. David P. Gauthier, *The Logic of Leviathan: The Moral and Political Theory of Thomas Hobbes* (Oxford: Clarendon, 1969), is an excellent secondary discussion.

Interest in the Social Contract Theory has been revived among contemporary philosophers largely through the work of the Harvard philosopher John Rawls. Rawls's *A Theory of Justice* (Cambridge, Mass.: Harvard University Press, 1971), which argues for a kind of contractarian theory, was the most acclaimed work of moral philosophy in the past three decades. Critical assessments of Rawls may be found in: Brian Barry, *The Liberal Theory of Justice* (Oxford: Oxford University Press, 1973); Robert Paul Wolff, *Understanding Rawls* (Princeton: Princeton University Press, 1977); and Norman Daniels, ed., *Reading Rawls* (New York: Basic Books, n.d.). David Gauthier's *Morals by Agreement* (Oxford: Oxford University Press, 1986) is also a major contribution to social contract theory.

On civil disobedience, see the essays collected in *Civil Disobedience: Theory and Practice*, edited by Hugo Adam Bedau (New York: Pegasus Books, 1969).

Chapter 12: The Ethics of Virtue

The classic work with which to begin is Aristotle's *Nicomachean Ethics*. Martin Ostwald's translation (Indianapolis: Bobbs-Merrill, 1962) is one of many available. Some of the most important recent books are: Philippa Foot, *Virtues and Vices and Other Essays in Moral Philosophy* (Berkeley: University of California Press, 1978); James D. Wallace, *Virtues and Vices* (Ithaca: Cornell University Press, 1978); and Edmund L. Pincoffs, *Quandaries and Virtues: Against Reductivism in Ethics* (Lawrence: University of Kansas Press, 1986).

Alasdair MacIntyre's *After Virtue* (Notre Dame: University of Notre Dame Press, 1981) is a seminal work; it is probably the most-discussed current treatment of the subject. MacIntyre's later volume *Whose Justice? Which Rationality?* (Notre Dame: University of Notre Dame Press, 1988) is a sequel.

The following articles are also recommended: Jonathan Bennett, "The Conscience of Huckleberry Finn," *Philosophy* 49 (1974), pp. 123–134; Michael Stocker, "The Schizophrenia of Modern Ethical Theories," *Journal of Philosophy* 73 (1976), pp. 453–466; Susan Wolf, "Moral Saints," *Journal of Philosophy* 79 (1982), pp. 419–439; and Robert Louden, "Some Vices of Virtue Ethics," *American Philosophical Quarterly* 21 (1984), pp. 227–236.

Gregory E. Pence, "Recent Work on the Virtues," *American Philosophical Quarterly* 21 (1984), pp. 281–297, is a helpful guide to work through 1984. Pence is also the author of the article on "Virtue Theory" in *A Companion to Ethics*, edited by Peter Singer (Oxford: Basil Blackwell, 1991), pp. 249–258.

An excellent collection of articles by various writers is *Midwest Studies in Philosophy, Vol. XII: Ethical Theory: Character and Virtue,* edited by Peter A. French, Theodore E. Uehling, Jr., and Howard K. Wettstein (Notre Dame: University of Notre Dame Press, 1988). Martha C. Nussbaum's "Non-Relative Virtues: An Aristotelian Approach," in this volume, is especially recommended. Another good collection is *Identity, Character, and Morality,* edited by Owen Flanagan and Amélie Oksenberg Rorty (Cambridge, Mass.: Bradford Books, 1990).

Chapter 13: What Would a Satisfactory Moral Theory Be Like?

On the need for a more modest conception of the moral "importance" of humankind, see James Rachels, *Created from Animals: The Moral Implications of Darwinism* (Oxford: Oxford University Press, 1990).

For more on desert, see J. Rachels, "What People Deserve," in *Justice and Economic Distribution,* edited by John Arthur and William H. Shaw (Englewood Cliffs, N.J.: Prentice-Hall, 1978).

Douglas Lackey's *Moral Principles and Nuclear Weapons* (Totowa, N.J.: Roman and Allenheld, 1984) is an excellent introduction to the moral issues surrounding nuclear strategy. See also Jan Narveson, "At Arm's Length: Violence and War," in *Matters of Life and Death,* edited by Tom Regan, 3rd ed. (New York: McGraw-Hill, 1993).

On "reverse discrimination," see the articles contained in *Equality and Preferential Treatment,* edited by Marshall Cohen, Thomas Nagel, and Thomas Scanlon (Princeton: Princeton University Press, 1977). For a longer treatment, Alan Goldman's book *Justice and Reverse Discrimination* (Princeton: Princeton University Press, 1979) is recommended.

Notes on Sources

The following account of my sources is a substitute for the more traditional apparatus of footnotes. Footnotes have not been used because in a book such as this they are of minimum interest to most readers, and they tend to clutter the text, making it less pleasant to read. Those interested in tracking down a quotation or reference will find sufficient information here to allow them to do so.

Chapter 1: What Is Morality?

The quotation from Dr. Anthony Shaw is from his article "Dilemmas of 'Informed Consent' in Children," *New England Journal of Medicine,* vol. 289 (1973), p. 886.

The quotation from Dr. Newman is from Gregory E. Pence, *Classic Cases in Medical Ethics* (New York: McGraw-Hill, 1990), p. 144.

The quotations from Dr. C. Everett Koop were taken from the article by Peter Singer and Helga Kuhse, "The Future of Baby Doe," *New York Review of Books,* March 1, 1984.

Chapter 2: The Challenge of Cultural Relativism

The story of the Greeks and the Callatians is from Herodotus, *The Histories,* translated by Aubrey de Selincourt, revised by A. R. Burn (Harmondsworth, Middlesex: Penguin Books, 1972), pp. 219–220. The quotation from Herodotus toward the end of the chapter is from the same source.

Information about the Eskimos was taken from Peter Freuchen, *Book of the Eskimos* (New York: Fawcett, 1961); and E. Adamson Hoebel, *The Law of Primitive Man* (Cambridge: Harvard University Press, 1954), Chapter 5. The estimate of how female infanticide affects the male/female ratio in the adult Eskimo population is from Hoebel's work.

The William Graham Sumner quotation is from his *Folkways* (Boston: Ginn and Company, 1906), p. 28.

Chapter 3: Subjectivism in Ethics

The C. L. Stevenson quotation is from his *Ethics and Language* (New Haven: Yale University Press, 1944), p. 114.

Chapter 4: Does Morality Depend on Religion?

The information about Governor Cuomo's ethics panel, and the quotation from the governor, are from the *New York Times*, October 4, 1984, p. 1.

The Bertrand Russell quotation is from his essay "A Free Man's Worship," *Mysticism and Logic* (Garden City, N.Y.: Doubleday, Anchor Books, n.d.), pp. 45–46.

Antony Flew makes the remark about philosophical talent in his *God and Philosophy* (New York: Dell, 1966), p. 109.

The Leibniz quotation is from his *Discourse on Metaphysics* (1686), which may be found in G. W. von Leibniz, *Philosophical Papers and Letters*, edited and translated by Leroy E. Loemker (Chicago: University of Chicago Press, 1956), vol. I, pp. 465–466.

The quotations from St. Thomas Aquinas are from the *Summa Theologica*, 1a–2ac, xviii, 8; xix, 5; and III *Quodlibet*, 27—translated by Thomas Gilby in *St. Thomas Aquinas: Philosophical Texts* (New York: Oxford University Press, 1960).

Chapter 5: Psychological Egoism

Hobbes's definitions of "charity" and "pity" are from *On Human Nature*, Chapter 9, parts 9 and 17; contained in vol. IV of the Molesworth edition of *The English Works of Thomas Hobbes* (London, 1845).

The story about Abraham Lincoln is from the *Springfield* (Ill.) *Monitor*, quoted by Frank Sharp in his *Ethics* (New York: Appleton-Century, 1928), p. 75.

For information about the Rosenham study, see David L. Rosenham, "On Being Sane in Insane Places," in *Labelling Madness*, edited by Thomas J. Scheff (Englewood Cliffs, N.J.: Prentice-Hall, 1975), pp. 54–74.

Chapter 6: Ethical Egoism

The quotations from Ayn Rand are from her book *The Virtue of Selfishness* (New York: Signet, 1964), pp. 27, 32, 80, and 81.

The quotation from Kurt Baier is from his book *The Moral Point of View* (Ithaca, N.Y.: Cornell University Press, 1958), pp. 189–190.

Chapter 7: The Utilitarian Approach

The opening quotation from Bentham is from his *Principles of Morals and Legislation* (New York: Hafner, 1948), p. 2. The quotation concerning animals is from the same work, p. 311.

The quotations from Mill are from his *Utilitarianism* (Indianapolis: Bobbs-Merrill, 1957), p. 16; and *On Liberty* (Indianapolis: Bobbs-Merrill, 1956), p. 13.

The case of Matthew Donnelly is taken from Robert M. Veatch, *Case Studies in Medical Ethics* (Cambridge: Harvard University Press, 1977), p. 328.

The quotations from Aquinas about animals are from *Summa Theologica*, II, II, Q. 64, Art. 6; and *Summa Contra Gentiles*, III, II, 12. See *Basic Writings of Saint Thomas Aquinas*, edited by Anton C. Pegis, 2 vols. (New York: Random House, 1945).

Singer describes the experiment with the forty dogs in *Animal Liberation* (New York: New York Review Books, 1975), p. 38. His discussion of the treatment of farm animals is in the same book, Chapter 3.

Chapter 8: The Debate over Utilitarianism

The quotation from Mill about impartiality is from *Utilitarianism* (Indianapolis: Bobbs-Merrill, 1957), p. 22.

McCloskey's example of the utilitarian tempted to bear false witness is from his paper "A Non-Utilitarian Approach to Punishment," *Inquiry*, vol. 8 (1965), pp. 239–255.

The J. J. C. Smart quotation is from J. J. C. Smart and Bernard Williams, *Utilitarianism: For and Against* (Cambridge: Cambridge University Press, 1973), p. 68.

Chapter 9: Are There Absolute Moral Rules?

Kant's statement of The Categorical Imperative is from his *Foundations of the Metaphysics of Morals,* translated by Lewis White Beck (Indianapolis: Bobbs-Merrill, 1959), p. 39.

The Elizabeth Anscombe quotation is from "Modern Moral Philosophy," *Philosophy,* vol. 33 (1958), p. 3.

Kant's "On a Supposed Right to Lie from Altruistic Motives" can be found in *Critique of Practical Reason and Other Writings in Moral Philosophy,* translated by Lewis White Beck (Chicago: University of Chicago Press, 1949). The quotation is from p. 348.

The P. T. Geach quotation is from his *God and the Soul* (London: Routledge and Kegan Paul, 1969), p. 128.

Chapter 10: Kant and Respect for Persons

Kant's remarks on animals are from his *Lectures on Ethics,* translated by Louis Infield (New York: Harper & Row, 1963), pp. 239–240.

The second formulation of The Categorical Imperative, in terms of treating persons as ends, is in *Foundations of the Metaphysics of Morals,* translated by Lewis White Beck (Indianapolis: Bobbs-Merrill, 1959), p. 47. The remarks about "dignity" and "price" are on p. 53.

Bentham's statement "All punishment is mischief" is from *The Principles of Morals and Legislation* (New York: Hafner, 1948), p. 170.

The quotations from Kant on punishment are from *The Metaphysical Elements of Justice,* translated by John Ladd (Indianapolis: Bobbs-Merrill, 1965), pp. 99–107, except for the quotation about the "right good beating," which is from *Critique of Practical Reason,* translated by Lewis White Beck (Chicago: University of Chicago Press, 1949), p. 170.

Karl Menninger's views are quoted from his article, "Therapy, Not Punishment," *Harper's Magazine* (August 1959), pp. 63–64.

Chapter 11: The Idea of a Social Contract

Hobbes's estimate of the state of nature is from his *Leviathan,* Oakeshott edition (Oxford: Blackwell, 1960), Chapter 13. The quotation is from p. 82.

The Rousseau quotation is from *The Social Contract and Discourses,* translated by G. D. H. Cole (New York: Dutton, 1959), pp. 18–19.

The quotations from King and Waldman may be found in *Civil Disobedience: Theory and Practice,* edited by Hugo Adam Bedau (New York: Pegasus Books, 1967), pp. 76–77, 78, 106, and 107.

The passage from Fontaine's memoirs is quoted in Peter Singer, *Animal Liberation* (New York: New York Review Books, 1975), p. 220.

Chapter 12: The Ethics of Virtue

The quotations from Aristotle are from Book II of the *Nicomachean Ethics*, translated by Martin Ostwald (Indianapolis: Bobbs-Merrill, 1962), except for the quotation about friendship, which is from Book VIII, and the quotation about visiting foreign lands, which is Martha C. Nussbaum's translation, given in her article "Non-Relative Virtues: An Aristotelian Approach," in *Midwest Studies in Philosophy, Vol. XII: Ethical Theory: Character and Virtue*, edited by Peter A. French, Theodore E. Uehling, Jr., and Howard K. Wettstein (Notre Dame: University of Notre Dame Press, 1988), pp. 32–53.

Peter Geach's remarks concerning courage are from his book *The Virtues* (Cambridge: Cambridge University Press, 1977), pp. xxix, xxx. The story about St. Athanasius appears on p. 114.

Plato's *Euthyphro* is available in several translations; a useful one is Hugh Tredennick's in Plato, *The Last Days of Socrates* (Harmondsworth, Middlesex: Penguin Books, revised edition 1959).

Pincoffs's suggestion about the nature of virtue appears in his book *Quandaries and Virtues: Against Reductivism in Ethics* (Lawrence: University of Kansas Press, 1986), p. 78.

The Nietzsche quotation is from Part Five of his *Beyond Good and Evil*, trans. Walter Kaufmann (New York: Vintage Books, 1966).

Michael Stocker's example is from his article "The Schizophrenia of Modern Ethical Theories," *Journal of Philosophy* 73 (1976), pp. 453–466.

The quotation from Mill is from *Utilitarianism* (Indianapolis: Bobbs-Merrill, 1957), p. 22.

Anscombe's proposal that the notion of "morally right" be jettisoned is made in her influential article "Modern Moral Philosophy," first published in *Philosophy* 33 (1958) and conveniently reprinted in *Ethics, Religion and Politics: The Collected Philosophical Papers of G. E. M. Anscombe*, vol. III (Minneapolis: University of Minnesota Press, 1981).

Chapter 13: What Would a Satisfactory Moral Theory Be Like?

Hume's statement about the universe not caring for us is from his essay "Of Suicide," which is conveniently reprinted in *Hume's Ethical Writings*, edited by Alasdair MacIntyre (New York: Collier, 1965), pp. 297–306. The quotation is from p. 301.

Index

Index